Tamana Aziz is a Director in the Private and Business Immigration department at Duncan Lewis Solicitors. Since joining the firm in January 2018, she has built upon a distinguished career spanning over two decades, having provided immigration advice and assistance since 2001.

Tamana advises on a wide array of immigration matters, including business immigration, high-net-worth individual cases, skilled worker extensions, spouse and visit visa applications, Global Talent visas, and British citizenship. Her practice is distinguished by its depth in complex litigation; she regularly appears before the Immigration Tribunals, the High Court, the Court of Appeal, and the Supreme Court in matters involving deportation appeals and country guidance cases.

Her expertise extends to both individual and corporate clients. She is a trusted advisor to employers and external organisations, delivering bespoke training on Home Office compliance, including the Prevention of Illegal Working Regime and the online sponsorship management system. Internally, she is responsible for training solicitors across Duncan Lewis on a variety of immigration law topics.

Recognised for her handling of high-profile, complex litigation—including matters that have reached the Supreme Court—Tamana is frequently sought after by the media. She appears regularly on television, radio, and in the UK press to provide expert legal commentary. Her courtroom advocacy has been judicially recognised; she was described as "an admirable solicitor and advocate" by the Court of Appeal in the landmark case of *HS Afghanistan*.

Tamana holds a Supervisor and Level 2 Senior Caseworker accreditation under the Law Society's Immigration and Asylum Accreditation Scheme. She is also instructed as an expert by local authorities, social services, and family lawyers to provide opinions on the immigration status of children and parents involved in care proceedings.

In addition to her practice, Tamana is deeply committed to legal education and mentorship. She is a contributor to the legal textbook Immigration Law and Practice, published in collaboration with CILEX Education and former Immigration Judge Richard McKee. She authored three chapters (13, 14, and 15), focusing on the essential attributes and practices of an effective immigration lawyer. She serves as an official mentor for students at the University of Westminster's Law School and runs pro bono clinics with King's College London and the Afghanistan and Central Asia Association.

Tamana is recognised as a leading practitioner in the legal directories. She is a 'Recommended Individual' in The Legal 500 2026, where she is described as "the all-rounder rockstar. She is incredibly knowledgeable, experienced and solution-driven… excellent in advising commercial clients on the immigration/employment law crossover." She is also ranked in Chambers UK 2026, where sources note: "Tamana has excellent and in-depth understanding, always aware of the trends and legislations, and is very professional."

A Practical Guide to UK Partner Route Visa for Immigration Lawyers

A Practical Guide to UK Partner Route Visa for Immigration Lawyers

Tamana Aziz

Law Brief Publishing

Published 2026 by Law Brief Publishing, an imprint of Law Brief Publishing Ltd
30 The Parks
Minehead
Somerset
TA24 8BT

www.lawbriefpublishing.com

Paperback: 978-1-918241-30-3

CONTENTS

INTRODUCTION

Spouse visas in the United Kingdom, officially categorised under Family Visa, provide a legal pathway for non-UK nationals to live and eventually settle in the UK with a partner who is a British citizen or settled in the UK

UK spouse visas originated from general family immigration rules, but became significantly stricter with the introduction of the minimum income requirement in July 2012, part of coalition government efforts to reduce net migration and prevent families from relying on public funds. This rule, initially £18,600, required sponsors (UK citizens/settled persons) to prove they could financially support their foreign spouses, alongside proving a genuine relationship and English language skills for applicants, evolving over time with significant increases to the threshold.

The origin goes back to 1976, one of the many pamphlets exposed the difficulties faced by migrants trying to enter the UK in the 1970s and 1980s. Several articles have been published since July 2012 when the income threshold was introduced, discussing the families potentially divided, such as an article by Richard Fabb in The Guardian.[1]

Being in immigration practice for the past 20 years, it has been a challenge navigating the immigration rules. Many of our clients have real stories to tell, particularly women who have been divided by the immigration control system and the strict requirements placed upon the applications for leave to enter and remain.

A pamphlet by Anne Owers titled 'Families Divided' from 1984 states:-

---

1 https://www.theguardian.com/commentisfree/2013/jul/09/uk-australia-spouse-visa

> *"It is often impossible to produce the sort of evidence which entry clearance officers will accept. Marriage and birth certificates rarely exist… Application forms have to completed in English…*
>
> *The interview itself can cause fresh problems… The purpose of the interview is to detect 'discrepancies' in family members' accounts… In other words, there is an assumption that the family is lying and questioning will reveal this."*

In the past 40 years the system has become tighter and tougher with new multiple new legislation being introduced in a short span of time to tighten immigration control.

A document in the Runnymede Trust archive files that is an internal circular for the British Embassy in Islamabad, Pakistan outlined the requirements for a spousal visa in 1976 ('Wives Wishing to Join or Accompany Husbands for Settlement in the United Kingdom', May 1976, RC/RF/1/06, Runnymede Trust archive, Black Cultural Archives, London). This document showed the requirements is set forth by the UKBA.

In 1976, the requirements for a spousal visa were that an applicant must provide the following:-

> *(a) A valid passport issued to the applicant.*
>
> *(b) Evidence that the husband is settled in the United Kingdom in the form of a declaration of sponsorship giving the husband's full name, his address, details of his employment, passport details and the date of his entry into the United Kingdom.*
>
> *(c) Evidence that a marriage has taken place…*
>
> *(d) Any recent family correspondence relating to the applicant proposed settlement in the United Kingdom.*

(e) Two passport size photographs of the applicant.

(f) Attested photocopies of the sponsor's passport. If the sponsor holds a British Passport photocopies of pages 1 to 6 inclusive and all other pages bearing frontier stamps should be produced. If the sponsor holds a [non-UK] passport complete photocopies of all passports in his possession should be produced. All copies should be attested on each page by a responsible person in the United Kingdom (a Notary Public, Commissioner of Oaths, or Solicitor) as being true copies of the original documents.

(g) Evidence that the husband is willing and able to support and accommodate his wife.

(Paragraph (g) does not apply to cases where the sponsor was, on 1 January, 1973, a Commonwealth Citizen settled in the United Kingdom).

The burden is always on the applicant to proof that the above requirements are met with benefit of doubt given to the applicant otherwise for the decision maker to disapprove any claims.

Legislative History

The foundation of modern UK spouse visas was built on several key acts:

- **Immigration Act 1971**: Established the concept of "settlement" and "Right of Abode," creating a formal structure for family reunification that took full effect on January 1, 1973.

- **British Nationality Act 1981**: Effective from 1983, this act removed the automatic right of foreign wives of British men to acquire citizenship, treating all foreign spouses equally under the law for the first time.

- **2012 Immigration Reform**: Introduced **Appendix FM** to the Immigration Rules, which implemented the first "Minimum Income Requirement" (MIR) of £18,600 to ensure families could support themselves without public funds

Modern Framework (2024–2026)

The spouse visa system has undergone significant transformation as of 2026:

- **Minimum Income Requirement**: In April 2024, the threshold for new applicants was raised from £18,600 to **£29,000**. This figure remains in place in 2026 while the government reviews recommendations from the Migration Advisory Committee.

- **Cash Savings Alternative**: Applicants who do not meet the income threshold can rely on cash savings. For the £29,000 threshold, the required savings amount is **£88,500**.

- **Pathway to Settlement**: Initial visas are typically granted for 2 years and 9 months. After living in the UK for a total of **5 years** on this route, spouses may apply for Settlement.

Modern Immigration Border controls originated in 1905 although some means of controlling foreign visitors to the United Kingdom existed before then. Although an Alien Act was passed in 1793 and remained in force to some extent until 1836, there were no controls between then and 1905 barring a very loosely policed system of registration on entry.

The legislation that finally emerged was the Aliens Act 1905. It was easily evaded, and did not even require Immigration Officers to give written permission to land or stamp a passport. Permission to land was given verbally.[2]

In this book I will outline a practical and easy guide to practitioners navigating spouse/partner applications. It will allow you to advise applicants in their applications and compile the necessary documentary evidence in support of their applications which is key to a successful application.

The stated law is up to date as of 24th March 2026.

2 https://en.wikipedia.org/wiki/History_of_UK_immigration_control

CHAPTER ONE

THE IMMIGRATION RULES AND REALITIES

In UK immigration Rules Appendix FM, a 'partner' is a person applying to join a British citizen or settled person in the UK, defined as a **spouse, civil partner, or an unmarried partner in a relationship similar to marriage/civil partnership for at least two years**, with recent changes clarifying the 'unmarried partner' criteria to focus on the relationship's nature rather than strict cohabitation. The rules (Appendix FM) detail requirements for family visas, covering financial, relationship, and suitability aspects for partners to join their sponsor in the UK. The rules are governed under "Appendix FM partner" introduced in July 2012, in essence it refers to someone seeking a family visa to join their partner (spouse, Civil partner or long term unmarried partner) under specific detailed immigration rules.

The part of the rules that applicants need to navigate are "Appendix FM[3]" (FM stands for family members) and "Appendix FM SE[4]. The rules are not easy to read, you need to navigate through them thoroughly the paragraphs are not numbered and somehow confusing.

For the practitioner, navigating spouse visa applications is not merely about form-filling; it's about strategic navigation within a complex, adversarial system. This chapter establishes the foundational map. We move beyond the public-facing 'Guidance' to examine the operative

3 https://www.gov.uk/guidance/immigration-rules/immigration-rules-appendix-fm-family-members

4 https://www.gov.uk/guidance/immigration-rules/immigration-rules-appendix-fm-se-family-members-specified-evidence

architecture: the Immigration Rules, their hidden tripwires, the caseworker culture that applies them, and the legal principles that govern them. Mastery here is the difference between a procedurally correct application and a strategically robust one.

Appendix FM (Family Members): This is the substantive rulebook. Section E-ECP (Entry Clearance as a Partner) and Section R-LTRP (Requirements for Leave to Remain as a Partner) contain the mandatory eligibility rules for the relationship, financial, accommodation, and language requirements. Know them verbatim. This can easily be divided into two parts suitability "criteria" and "eligibility criteria". Suitability looks at your client's character to assess if there are reasons why they should not be admitted to or allowed to remain in the UK. There are mandatory and discretionary grounds to refuse applications for suitability reasons. Mandatory grounds mean that Home Office officials must reject the visa application for this reason. Discretionary grounds mean that they "will normally" or "may" reject the application but may choose not to. In some instances it is very likely that they will, in others less so. The main reasons why an application will be refused concern criminality, such as being the subject of a deportation order, or having been convicted of an offence and sentenced to a period of imprisonment of at least four years.

In case of sentences between one and four years, the application will be refused unless a period of ten years has passed from the end of the sentence. For sentences of less than 12 months, the person will need to wait for five years before applying.[5]

Even in the absence of any conviction, there are circumstances that will lead to a refusal if the Home Office is satisfied that the exclusion of the applicant is "conducive to the public good". This wording is in paragraph

5 https://freemovement.org.uk/how-to-apply-for-uk-spouse-partner-visa-appendix-fm/

S-EC1.5, which says that an example of what is not conducive to the public good is where the applicant's

> "*character, associations, or other reasons, make it undesirable to grant them entry clearance*"

In UK Immigration law, **Paragraph S-EC1.5 of Appendix FM** to the Immigration Rules is a mandatory ground for refusal of an application for entry clearance (EC).

It states that the exclusion of an applicant from the UK is conducive to the public good because, for example, the applicant's:

- conduct (including convictions that do not fall within the scope of more serious mandatory refusal grounds)
- character
- associations
- or other reasons

...make it undesirable to grant them entry clearance. This is a discretionary power used by the Entry Clearance Officer (ECO) or Secretary of State to refuse a visa even if specific, serious criminality thresholds are not met. This was covered under part 9.[6] Grounds for refusal which was a gate keeper. the relevant paragraphs in Part 9 of the main Immigration Rules are paragraphs 320(7A) and 7(B) for entry clearance, as well as paragraph 322(1A) for leave to remain applications.

Paragraphs 320(7A) and 322(1A) have the effect of causing any application in which deception is used to be refused. Paragraph

6 https://www.gov.uk/guidance/immigration-rules

320(7B)(d) combined with (ii) causes future entry clearance applications to be refused for ten years.

In particular, paragraph 320(7A) states that an application is to be refused:

where false representations have been made or false documents or information have been submitted (whether or not material to the application, and whether or not to the applicant's knowledge), or material facts have not been disclosed, in relation to the application or in order to obtain documents from the Secretary of State or a third party required in support of the application.

Example:- Alex has submitted an application for leave to enter the UK as an unmarried partner of a British citizen. He submitted an English certificate which turns out to be counterfeit. Alex explains that his application was submitted through an agent and he did not know that the document was counterfeit. Even if the entry clearance officer believes Alex, they will have to refuse the application under paragraph 320 7 (A) on the basis that a false document was submitted.

Discretionary Refusals

As a well as the automatic or mandatory refusals on deception grounds there are a number of provisions which permit an entry clearance officer or Home Office official to refuse an application for current or past deception. It should not be assumed that there is any reluctance to exercise these powers; the wording of many of these rules is that entry clearance "should normally be refused". This means there is a presumption that the application will be refused.

Paragraph 320(11) of the Immigration Rules is one example of this type of rule. It says an application should **normally** be refused:

(11) where the applicant has previously contrived in a significant way to frustrate the intentions of the Rules by:

[...](iv) using deception in an application for entry clearance, leave to enter or remain or in order to obtain documents from the Secretary of State or a third party required in support of the application (whether successful or not); and there are other aggravating circumstances, such as absconding, not meeting temporary admission/reporting restrictions or bail conditions, using an assumed identity or multiple identities, switching nationality, making frivolous applications or not complying with the re-documentation process.

This rule applied to Appendix FM as well as to other types of application and is sometimes used to refuse applicants with a very poor immigration history in the UK.

Practitioners must try to avoid mistakes that can be interpreted as deception, it can be a small mistake such as ticking a box incorrectly on the application form or forgetting to mention previous immigration history. The main type of accidental "deception" I have come across in my line of work are:-

- Failure to mention previous marriage and or minor conviction
- Wrong answers about previous refusals
- Allegation of use of False document

It is important to understand that any conviction be it small such as driving offences, cautions are still a criminal conviction. It is important not to associate a conviction to merely a criminal sentence.

Sometimes your client's applications can be refused when the Entry clearance officer or home Office alleges that a false document has been used in their applications, the first step as practitioner should take is to request a document verification report (DVR)[7] from the decision maker. A DVR is a document which can be produced by the person verifying a document. A DVR should give a better idea of what the allegation is and whether there was a misunderstanding. It also makes it clearer what kind of evidence should be gathered to rebut the allegation that a document was false. Take an example of a refusal which is based on submissions of wrong tax returns where a DVR showed that the national insurance number did not match those of the sponsor.

Deception has to be deliberate. The court of appeal has held that a deliberate intention to deceive is needed when refusing under paragraph 322 (1A) of the immigration rules.

In the case of *R (Agha) v Secretary of State for the Home Department (False document)* [2017] UKUT 121(IAC)[8], the Upper Tribunal found that:-

For a document to be a false document under the provision of the Immigration Rules at V3.6(a) of Appendix V I find, relying on *AA (Nigeria)*, there must have been an element of dishonesty in its creation and if this is not immediately obvious in a case of an inaccurate document then that element must be engaged with in any refusal.

When immigration officers want to refuse the application also on the basis that the applicant used deception, therefore imposing a ten-year re-entry ban, deception must come from the applicant. The immigration tribunal has addressed the issue in many cases, generally interpreting the mandatory refusal grounds in an appropriately restrictive way given their draconian consequences.

7 https://www.gov.uk/government/publications/document-verification-checks

8 https://www.bailii.org/uk/cases/UKUT/IAC/2017/121.html

In the case of *Ozhogina and Tarasova (deception within para 320(7B) – nannies) Russia* [2011] UKUT 197 (IAC)[9], Mr Justice Burton also concluded that:-

> *25. […] for the purpose of qualifying for the ten year treatment under paragraph 320(7B) the nannies must be shown to have made the false statements with the deliberate intent of securing advantage in immigration terms.*

As a practitioner you must takes step and avoid bans based on deception this means:

- Double checking application forms before they are submitted; many clients will tell you that their applications were submitted through agents. This is never a valid reason to submit false or inaccurate information, and the Home Office will always hold them responsible for any information contained in the form, as they did, at the end of the day, sign the form.

- Paying close attention to potential problem questions, like previous convictions and previous immigration history (see above). If in doubt as to whether an issue that arose in the past will be considered a conviction, it would be a good idea to raise it in the application. It is often better to disclose more than less.

- Checking passports to make sure the applicant has not forgotten anything and has given correct dates in relation to past travel history.

- Telling the truth!

---

9 https://www.bailii.org/uk/cases/UKUT/IAC/2011/00197_ukut_iac_2011_nat_others_russia.html

Nevertheless, accidents happen and sometimes applicants are refused for deception either because of a mistake or a misunderstanding. In these cases, the applicants can (and should be encouraged to) challenge the refusal by submitting new evidence explaining why and how a mistake was made. Applicants should be particularly encouraged to challenge decisions when these attract a ten-year re-entry ban.

There is also this common sense guidance to immigration officials, thanks to a Freedom of Information Request:-

> *The ECO needs to be satisfied that deception has been employed and/or the applicant intended to deceive the ECO. The majority of cases where this requires the ECOs judgement will relate to how an applicant has completed the VAF, most usually in relation to the questions about previous visa refusals or the grant or refusal of Leave to Remain (LTR). A prime example of this is when an applicant ticks the wrong box on the VAF in answer to the question 'have you previously been refused a visa' – e.g. an applicant has ticked that they have not previously been refused a UK visa, but has presented a passport containing a refusal stamp and/or a previous refusal notice. This should not be considered to be deception – therefore paragraph 320 7 (a) should not apply.*

The source is OPI 177 issued in 2009,[10] released under Freedom of Information request 19343/20435/23557 by the Foreign and Commonwealth Office.

Part 9 of the Immigration Rules, which previously contained the general grounds for refusal, has undergone significant changes. As of 11 November 2025, Part Suitability replaced Part 9 and now applies to most immigration routes, including Appendix FM applications. This marks a

10 https://freemovement.org.uk/wp-content/uploads/2013/10/OPI-177-issued-2009.pdf

shift from the previous position where Appendix FM had its own suitability requirements, which were, in some cases, more lenient than those under Part 9.

It is important to note that the suitability requirements under Appendix FM do not adopt all the provisions of Part 9. For instance, paragraph A320 of the Immigration Rules explicitly excludes the application of certain provisions of Part 9 to Appendix FM applications, reflecting Parliament's intention to maintain distinct and not incorporate all the grounds for refusal under part 9. Specific provisions under Appendix FM (suitability) continue to apply to these applications which will be explored further in this book.

It is crucial to approach every case with a dual lens such as the compliance lens (checking every box in Appendix FM) and the adversarial lens (anticipating how a pressured caseworker might misread or doubt your evidence). Your role is to build a bridge between your client's circumstances and the Immigration Rules so robust that the only possible outcome is a grant.

CHAPTER TWO

PARTNERS – RELATIONSHIP REQUIREMENT

In 2026, the relationship requirements for a UK visa under Appendix FM focuses on ensuring the partnership is authentic, legally recognized (where applicable), and durable.[11]

The relationship requirements under Appendix FM of the Immigration Rules are essential for partner applications. These requirements ensure that the applicant and their sponsoring partner meet specific criteria to establish a genuine and subsisting relationship. In your practice the first element of any application will start by meeting the relationship requirement.

Appendix FM of the Immigration Rules governs applications for leave to enter or remain in the UK as a partner. The relationship requirements under Appendix FM are designed to ensure that the applicant and their sponsoring partner have a genuine and subsisting relationship, meet specific eligibility criteria, and intend to live permanently in the UK. The requirements include meeting in person, not being in a prohibited degree of relationship, providing evidence of a genuine and subsisting relationship, demonstrating the permanent breakdown of any previous relationships, and showing an intention to live permanently in the UK.

What is relationship? a relationship is defined in legal not just emotional terms.

---

[11] https://www.gov.uk/guidance/immigration-rules/immigration-rules-appendix-fm-family-members

A relationship means:-

"***a genuine and subsisting partnership between two people who intend to live together permanently***" evidence by commitment and shared life arrangements. The terms are broken down in immigration rules and the Home Office is looking for genuine, subsisting, recognised partner status, exclusivity and intention to live together. We will look at these in more depth in this chapter.

The following key terms used in the Immigration Rules in relation to applications by partners applying under Part 8 and Appendix FM of the Immigration Rules:

- •prohibited degree of relationship
- •present and settled
- •intention to live together permanently in the UK
- •have met in person
- •genuine and subsisting relationship
- •any previous relationship must have broken down permanently

This chapter focuses on issues which are more frequently encountered by the practitioners. It does not cover:

- •validity and recognition of marriages/civil partnerships
- •recognition of overseas divorces/civil partnership dissolutions
- •forced marriages

- •polygamous marriages

Comprehensive Home Office guidance on those issues can be found in the relevant Home Office guidance.[12]

Requirement to Meet in Person: The Immigration Rules, both in Part 8 and Appendix FM, require the applicant and sponsoring partner to have met in person. This requirement has been interpreted by the Tribunal to mean that the parties must have made each other's acquaintance, which does not necessarily need to be in the context of marriage or civil partnership.

The requirement for the applicant and sponsoring partner to have met in person is a fundamental aspect of Appendix FM. The Tribunal has clarified that this requirement means the parties must have made each other's acquaintance, which involves more than a mere mutual sighting or coming face-to-face. This interpretation ensures that the relationship is genuine and not solely based on virtual interactions. Evidence such as travel history, photographs, or communication records can be used to demonstrate compliance with this requirement.

The previous Entry Clearance Guidance suggested providing evidence of the meeting, such as travel history and relevant email exchanges. It is considered good practice to include details of the circumstances of the meeting(s) in the applicant's and sponsor's supporting statements. This ensures that the requirement is adequately demonstrated.

In the case of ***Mohd Meharban v Entry Clearance Officer, Islamabad,***[13] it was clarified that the parties to an arranged marriage must meet in person in the context of marriage or marriage arrangements. This meeting should involve an appreciation of each party by the other, such

---

12 See Marriage Act 1949 s 25. Matrimonial Causes Act 1973, s 11

13 Mohd Meharban v Entry Clearance Officer, Islamabad | Books | Butterworths Immigration Law Service

as their appearance or personality. The case highlighted that meeting through online platforms like Facebook or Skype does not fulfil the requirement of "meeting in person" under Appendix FM.

The parties to an arranged marriage need not necessarily have met, but this is a requirement of the Immigration Rules. Professor Jackson here clarifies that 'the parties should have met in the context of marriage or marriage arrangements'. This necessitates 'at least an appreciation of each party by the other in the sense of, for example, appearance or personality'. In the instant case, the parties had played together as children, but that was the limit of their acquaintance. They had not '*met*' within the meaning of the Rules.

Appendix FM now requires the parties to have met '*in person*', no doubt to make it clear that meeting on Facebook, Skype or other Internet sites is not good enough, even if it enables some impression to be obtained of the partner's appearance and personality.

In *J (Pakistan)* *[2003] UKAIT 167*[14], where the parties to the marriage had never met and the wedding was conducted over the telephone, the marriage itself was invalid.

There is no specific requirement in the rules to prove having met. The Entry Clearance Officers (ECO) rarely conduct interviews. It is therefore vital to provide good evidence that the couple have met at the time of application, such as returned tickets, hotel bookings, boarding passes, photographs together and in some instances witness statements from friends, family and those who acted as witnesses during the marriage ceremony.

14 **Appellant and Entry Clearance Officer* Islamabad Respondent, [2003] UKIAT00167

A Valid marriage

For a marriage to be recognised by the Home Office, it has to be valid under the law of the country where it was performed this is long established in private law ***see Berthiaume v Dastous [1930] accept 79.***[15] this means that even marriage arrangements where the one or both the parties are in the UK while the marriage is formalised in their country of origin must be recognised ***CB Brazil.***[16]

he marriage must be Monogamy, polygamous marriages are generally not recognised. You only need to consider the validity of the marriage or civil partnership at the person's first application as a partner of their current spouse or civil partner, unless there are grounds to think the previous decision that the marriage or civil partnership is valid was incorrect.

The purpose of this requirement is to ensure that marriages or civil partnerships are carried out in accordance with the law of the country in which they took place and are recognised in the UK. The Home Office gives detailed guidance of evidence of marriage and proxy marriage (Relationship with a partner 8/10/2024).[17]

It is also good practice where there isn't sufficient evidence of marriage being valid to advise the applicant to enter as a fiancé and once here register their marriage.

15 Eugene Berthiaume v Dame Anne-Marie Yvonne Dastous (Quebec) [1929] UKPC 73 (16 July 1929)

16 CB (Validity of marriage: proxy marriage) Brazil [2008] UKAIT 00080 (10 October 2008)

17 https://www.gov.uk/government/publications/relationship-with-a-partner-caseworker-guidance/relationship-with-a-partner-accessible#Valid_Marriage

Where an applicant has previously been married you must provide divorce papers or other evidence of divorce that was effective in the country it took place, the Home Office Guidance Relationship with a partner notes that the fact of a new valid marriage may itself be accepted as evidence of termination of any previous marriage.[18]

Present and Settled in the UK

Present and settled simply means having legal immigration status as settled defined in rule 6 if the immigration rules having settlement, Indefinite leave to remain or a right of abode with physical presence in the UK. This also includes refugee sponsors with limited leave to remain and EEA national with a permanent right of residence in the UK.

Subsisting Relationship

Section **E-ECP.2.6**[19] states that the relationship between the applicant and their partner must be a genuine and subsisting relationship. As an applicant, it can be difficult to determine precisely what this means and in turn, this can make it difficult to determine what type of evidence you may wish to use in your application. The immigration guidance and application forms sheds some light on how caseworkers will assess if the relation between the partner and spouse is genuine and subsisting such as having financial commitments together, children in the picture, having proof of letters of correspondence address to the applicant and partner or in entry clearance cases travel to the partner's home country, providing chat records and phone bills.

18 Relationship with a partner

19 https://www.gov.uk/guidance/immigration-rules/immigration-rules-appendix-fm-family-members

In *Naz (subsisting marriage – standard of proof)* **[2012] UKUT 40**[20] the Entry Clearance Officer refused the application for the following reasons:

> *"It is reasonable to expect that in a genuine, subsisting, supporting and affectionate relationship…that there would be significant evidence of regular contact, signs of companionship, emotional support, affection, and abiding interest in each other's welfare and wellbeing…I am not satisfied that you have genuinely formed a relationship and durable with outward signs of affection and companionship."* – para. 3

The case establishes that the standard of proof is balance of probabilities such is regular communication however *Goudey (subsisting marriage – evidence) Sudan* **[2012] UKUT 00041 (IAC)**[21] it was established that it is not a requirement to have to text your partner.

Having said that it is vital in most of the applications that practitioners provide evidence of regular contact with each other such as WhatsApp chat records.

The Home Office guidance summaries relationship requirements and explains in more details of the requirements.[22]

In ***Kaur***,[23] the Upper Tribunal confirmed that a marriage could be genuine but not subsisting, hence why it is important to evidence your ongoing relationship with your partner. The couple were married, however they were physically separated and there was a lack of interaction

20 https://tribunalsdecisions.service.gov.uk/utiac/2012-ukut-40

21 https://tribunalsdecisions.service.gov.uk/utiac/2012-ukut-41

22 Relationship with a partner

23 https://tribunalsdecisions.service.gov.uk/utiac/oa-15204-2013

between them. It was determined that the test for 'subsisting' includes communication, emotional ties and intention to live together:

> *"The real issue in the case was whether the relationship between the appellant and sponsor continued to be one of mutual emotional support, companionship and an intention to resume or continue living together as husband and wife. That is the meaning to be attributed to the expression 'subsisting'"* – paragraph 13.

In *GA ("Subsisting" Marriage)* **[2006] UKAIT 46** the tribunal held that:

> *"An Immigration Judge, when assessing the subsistence of a marriage will plainly have to bear in mind the cultural context and the wide differences that exist between individual lifestyles, whether by choice, or by circumstances, or by economic necessity."* – paragraph 14.[24]

The Immigration Rules explicitly prohibit relationships within a prohibited degree of relationship, as defined by the Marriage Act 1949, the Marriage (Prohibited Degrees of Relationship) Act 1986, and the Civil Partnership Act 2004. This requirement ensures that the applicant and sponsor are not closely related in a way that would legally prohibit their relationship. Applicants must provide evidence to confirm that their relationship does not fall within these prohibited degrees.[25]

For all partner applications under Appendix FM, any previous relationship of the applicant or their partner must have permanently broken down. This requirement ensures that the applicant and sponsor are not in a concurrent relationship with another person. For unmarried partners, evidence must be provided to demonstrate the permanent breakdown of any previous relationship, even if the marriage or civil

---

24 https://tribunalsdecisions.service.gov.uk/utiac/2006-ukait-46

25 Partners, divorce and dissolution

partnership has not been legally dissolved. For fiancé(e)s and proposed civil partners, neither party can be married or in a civil partnership with another person at the time of application.

Appendix FM requires that the British citizen/settled sponsor and their applicant partner must intend to live permanently in the UK following the grant of leave. This requirement is distinct from the 'present and settled' requirement under Part 8 of the Immigration Rules. Evidence of this intention may include plans for accommodation, employment, or other arrangements in the UK.

Under Appendix FM of the UK Immigration Rules, the minimum age requirements are generally that **both the applicant and their partner (sponsor) must be 18 years of age or older** at the date of application. The supreme court in ***Quila***[26] found that an earlier rule change raising the minimum age to 21 was unlawful.

To conclude the relationship requirements under Appendix FM of the Immigration Rules are designed to ensure that partner applications are based on genuine and subsisting relationships. In doing your applications you must demonstrate that your client has met their sponsoring partner in person, are not in a prohibited degree of relationship, have a genuine and subsisting relationship, and that any previous relationships have permanently broken down. Additionally, the applicant and sponsor must intend to live permanently in the UK following the grant of leave. Compliance with these requirements is essential to avoid refusal of the application. Applicants should ensure that all necessary evidence is provided to substantiate their claims and address any potential issues that may arise during the application process.

---

26 R (on the application of Quila and another) (FC) (Respondents) v Secretary of State for the Home Department (Appellant) - UK Supreme Court

CHAPTER THREE

MAINTENANCE AND FINANCIAL REQUIREMENTS

The financial requirement is the single most common reason for refusal. For practitioners, it is not an arithmetic exercise but a forensic accounting and strategic planning challenge. This chapter moves beyond reciting the Rules (Appendix FM, Section FIN-SE) to the application of those Rules in complex, real-world scenarios. We focus on evidence architecture, risk mitigation, and strategic category selection to build an unassailable financial case. In Practise majority of appeals I have dealt with are based on not meeting the financial requirements of the immigration rules.

The immigration Rules are inflexible therefore the evidence must be immaculate, the court of appeal in ***Ahmed***[27] confirmed that there is no general "discretion" to waive the requirements. It is therefore important to present evidence the fits the purpose and prescribed category that you are relying on.

For most categories, income must be evidenced over a specific, continuous period prior to the application date. Calendar alignment is critical. A single day outside the specified period can invalidate the source. The Rules exclusively use gross income (before tax and National Insurance).

The Home Office demands specific documents listed in the Rules. A bank statement showing a salary deposit is not a substitute for a payslip.

---

27 https://www.bailii.org/uk/cases/UKUT/IAC/2013/00084_ukut_iac_2013_sa_bangladesh.html

Provide exactly what is mandated. We will look at each category that your clients may wish to rely on. We will also elaborate on those sponsors claiming state benefits and unable to show employment income.

The requirements are primarily divided into two main streams: employment/self-employment income and non-employment income/savings. The most common route is Category A or B income from salaried employment. The Home Secretary's plan to cut net Migration (fact Sheet[28]) brought a major change to the income threshold lifting the limit from £18600 to £29000.

There are transitional arrangements for those already on the Appendix FM route, providing they remain with the same partner. Applications made before 11 April 2024 will continue under the previous Rules. There is detailed guidance on minimum income requirements.[29] All earnings must be lawfully derived and to be assessed on a case-by-case *basis (Fatima [2002] UKUT 155 (IAC).*[30]

A. Income from Employment or Self-Employment

This is the most common method for meeting the requirement.

1. Category A: Salaried Employment (with current employer for 6+ months)

Applicant and/or sponsor has been with the same employer for at least 6 months at the date of application, earning a gross annual salary at or above the required threshold.

---

28 https://homeofficemedia.blog.gov.uk/2024/05/23/reducing-net-migration-factsheet-december-2023/

29 https://www.gov.uk/government/publications/chapter-8-appendix-fm-family-members

30 https://www.bailii.org/uk/cases/UKUT/IAC/2022/155.html

Under Category A, the applicant or their sponsoring partner must have been employed with the same employer for at least six months prior to the application. For salaried employment, the calculation is based on the lowest level of gross income during the six-month period. For non-salaried employment, the total income over the six months is divided by six to calculate the average monthly income, which is then multiplied by 12 to determine the annual income. If the sponsoring partner is returning to the UK from overseas, they must have a confirmed job offer with a gross annual income that meets the financial requirement, either alone or in combination with other permitted sources of income.

Additional sources of income can be combined to meet the financial requirement, including non-employment income, cash savings above £16,000, and pensions. However, cash savings must be held in an eligible format and controlled by the applicant or their partner for at least six months prior to the application. The savings cannot be borrowed and must be readily accessible. For example, to meet the £18,600 financial requirement solely through cash savings, a couple would need £34,600 for settlement applications or £62,500 for limited leave applications.

The evidence required to meet the Category A financial requirement includes pay slips, personal bank statements showing salary deposits, and a letter from the employer confirming the employment details, such as gross annual salary, length of employment, and type of employment. If the applicant or sponsor is employed outside the UK, equivalent evidence must be provided. For a sponsoring partner returning to the UK, a letter confirming the job offer, gross annual salary, and start date within three months of return is required.

It is important to ensure that all income and savings are lawfully derived and properly evidenced. The Immigration Rules specify detailed requirements for the format and content of the evidence, including bank statements, pay slips, and employer letters. Any documents not in English or Welsh must be accompanied by a certified translation.

2. Category B: Salaried Employment (with current employer for less than 6 months) / Variable Income

This category has two parts; you must meet either:-

Part 1 The current annual salary from employment (at the application date) must meet the financial threshold.

Part 2 The total gross salaried earnings from (any) employment in the 12 months prior to the application must meet the financial threshold.

This category is often used for those who have recently started a new job, have variable commissions/bonuses, or have changed jobs within the last year.

Under Category B, the financial requirement can be met in two ways. First, if the applicant or sponsoring partner is in the UK, the gross annual salary is calculated based on the current employment income. For salaried employment, the gross annual salary is determined from the pay slip or employment contract at the date of application. For non-salaried employment, the average gross income is calculated based on the period of employment held, using the following formula: total gross income divided by the number of months, weeks, or days worked, and then multiplied by 12, 52, or 365 respectively to give the annual salary.

Second, if the sponsoring partner is returning from overseas and is not yet employed in the UK, they must provide evidence of a confirmed offer of employment starting within three months of their return. The gross annual income from this offer must meet the financial requirement either alone or in combination with other eligible income sources, such as non-employment income, pensions, or cash savings above £16,000. However, cash savings cannot be combined with self-employment income under Categories F and G.

Additionally, the applicant must demonstrate that the financial requirement was met based on income earned in the 12 months prior to the date of application. This includes eligible employment income, non-employment income, and pensions, but excludes cash savings. The evidence required to support the application includes payslips, employment contracts, bank statements showing salary deposits, and employer letters confirming employment details.

To meet the financial requirement under Category B of Appendix FM, where the minimum income threshold is £29,000 per annum, the calculation depends on the applicant's employment history and income. Category B applies when the sponsor has been employed for less than six months with their current employer or has been self-employed for less than the last full financial year. The calculation involves assessing the total income earned in the last 12 months and ensuring it meets the required threshold.

For example, if a sponsor has been employed for four months with their current employer and earned a gross monthly salary of £2,500, their income for the four months would be £10,000. To meet the £29,000 threshold, the sponsor would need to demonstrate additional income from other sources, such as non-employment income, self-employment income, or cash savings. If the sponsor has £16,000 in cash savings, the formula under Appendix FM allows the sponsor to use savings above £16,000 to meet the shortfall. The shortfall in this case would be £19,000 (£29,000 - £10,000). The sponsor would need additional savings of £47,500 (calculated as £19,000 x 2.5) to meet the financial requirement

Alternatively, if the sponsor has been self-employed for less than a year and has accumulated gross earnings of £29,321, as evidenced by their annual self-assessment tax return, they would meet the financial requirement without needing to rely on additional sources of income or savings. This is consistent with the approach outlined in *Sultana and Others*, where the sponsor's self-employment income was used to meet the financial requirement *Sultana and Others (rules: waiver/further enquiry; discretion.* [31]

It is important to ensure that all specified evidence, such as pay slips, bank statements, and employer letters, is provided to demonstrate compliance with the financial requirements under Appendix FM-SE.

3. Self-Employment, Director of a Limited Company, or Business Person

Income is proven via the most recent full financial year's accounts (as submitted to HMRC).

Usually, the average of the last full financial year's taxable profit (as per Self-Assessment tax return) is used. For company directors, income can be a combination of salary (through PAYE) and dividends from the company. Requires extensive evidence: tax returns, tax year overviews, business accounts, proof of business registration, etc.

Appendix FM of the Immigration Rules outlines the financial requirements for family members seeking entry clearance or leave to remain in the UK. For self-employed individuals, the rules provide specific guidance on how their income is assessed and the evidence required to meet the minimum income threshold. Self-employed persons include sole traders, partners in partnerships (including limited partnerships and limited liability partnerships), and individuals in franchise agreements. However, the term "franchise agreement" is noted as being unrelated to employment or tax status, as it is a commercial arrangement between business entities. The key determinant for self-employment status under Appendix FM is whether the individual paid tax on a self-employed basis in the last financial year.

---

31 https://tribunalsdecisions.service.gov.uk/utiac/2014-ukut-540

The Immigration Rules also address certain anomalies regarding self-employment income. For example, equity partners in professional services firms, such as law firms, are treated as salaried employees for the purposes of Appendix FM, even though their income is derived from profit shares rather than fixed salaries. Additionally, directors and certain employees of specified limited companies are treated as self-employed for the purposes of meeting the financial requirements. Subcontractors under the Construction Industry Scheme have the option to classify their income as either self-employment or employment income.

Self-employed individuals can rely on income from the last full financial year (Category F) or an average of the last two full financial years (Category G) to meet the financial requirements under Appendix FM. If combining self-employment income with other sources, such as employment or pension income, the income from all sources must relate to the same financial year(s). Furthermore, evidence of ongoing self-employment or specified directorship / employment must be provided at the time of application. For applicants returning to the UK to continue self-employment, additional evidence is required, such as a signed contract for services, a partnership agreement, or proof of business premises acquisition.

The calculation of gross annual income for self-employed individuals includes income from self-employment, salaried or non-salaried employment, specified non-employment income, and pensions received by the applicant or their partner. However, self-employment income cannot be combined with specified savings to meet the minimum income threshold under Appendix FM see *Asma Begum.*[32]

This category is very complex and requires intensive examination of all the documents and tax records.

---

32 *Asma Begum v Secretary of State for the Home Department; Asma Begum (employment income; Rules/Article 8) Bangladesh* [2021] INLR 457

Definition of 'full financial year'

The relevant full financial year(s) for sole traders and partners will be that/those to which their last or last two self-assessment tax return(s) for which they have received a Statement(s) of Account from HMRC (SA300 or SA302) relate.

Note that it is possible for self-employed persons to have a different accounting period to the UK tax year, and for the accounting year which ended in their last tax year to form the basis of their tax liability for their last tax return. However, the relevant guidance provides that the relevant period for persons relying on self-employed income as a sole trader, partner 'or in a franchise' must be the period from 6 April in one year to 5 April the next. From November 2014 it has also stated that *'a sponsor wishing to rely on earnings from self-employment as a sole trader, as a partner or in a franchise will need to arrange to file their self-assessment tax return to HMRC on a timescale geared to meeting this requirement of the Immigration Rules rather than the deadline set for UK tax purposes'*. The tax return can include provisional figures, provided that additional evidence is provided to back these up. The guidance confirms that if the applicant is relying on the sponsoring partner's previous self-employment overseas, the relevant financial year(s) will be defined according to the requirements of the taxation system of that country.

For a director or (for applications decided on or after 6 April 2017) employee of a specified limited company in the UK, the relevant financial year(s) will be that/those covered by the company's Company Tax Return (CT 600) and will correspond with its last (2) 12-month accounting year(s).

In most cases, a company director who is also a shareholder will receive dividends and an employee (including an employed director) who is also a shareholder will receive a combination of salary and dividends. Salary (and in the case of non-executive directors fees in lieu of salary) can be relied on as employment income under Categories A or B. Dividends can be relied on under Category C (non-employment income).

Sole Traders and Partners

The immigration rules Appendix FM SE para 19 (b)B provides that a person's gross annual income from self-employment will be:

- •the gross taxable profits from their share of the business in the relevant financial year(s)
- •not including any deductible allowances, expenses or liabilities which may be applied to the gross taxable profits to establish the final tax liability.

In basic terms, in the UK, sole traders complete a tax return that will include the taxable profits (or losses) of their business in the accounting period that ends during the tax year to which the return relates. Taxable profits are calculated based on the total income less any expenses or allowances that can be deducted from the total figure.

Specified Evidence

The specified evidence for those relying on self-employment or specified directorship/employment income is quite extensive.

The below tables must be read in conjunction with the general requirements for the format of specified evidence, for which see home office guidance specified evidence.

Sole trader or partner

- Evidence of the amount of tax payable, paid and unpaid for the last full/last two full financial year(s)—eg Tax Year Overview produced by HMRC
- Annual self-assessment tax return(s) to HMRC for the last full/last two full financial year(s) (copy or printout)

Note: where the tax return includes provisional figures, the relevant guidance advises that a covering letter is also provided which confirms this and how the provisional figures and the figures given in the other evidence provided tie in with each other

- Statement(s) of Account (SA 300 or SA 302) for the last full/last two full financial year(s)

- Proof of registration with HMRC as self-employed (if available)

- Each partner's Unique Tax Reference Number (UTR) and/or the UTR of the partnership or business

- Where the person holds or held a separate business bank account(s), bank statements for the same 12-month/24-month period as the tax return(s)

- Personal bank statements for the same 12-month/24-month period as the tax return(s) showing that the income from self-employment has been paid into an account in the name of the person, or in the name of the person and their partner jointly, and

- Evidence of ongoing self-employment through until April 2016, evidence of payment of Class 2 National Insurance contributions (NICs) (unless the person has reached state pension age, and therefore is no longer required to pay Class 2 NICs, in which case evidence of their ongoing self-employment can be provided via alternative evidence, eg evidence of ongoing payment of business rates, business-related insurance premiums, employer NICs or franchise payments to the parent company) —from April 2016 to 23 November 2016, alternative evidence as detailed above or evidence of payment of some other business-related cost such as a licence to trade or a taxi licence, or bank statements showing ongoing receipt of self-employment income

—from 24 November 2016, at least one of the following documents: a bank statement dated no more than three months prior to the date of the application showing transactions relating to ongoing trading, or evidence dated no more than three months prior to the date of the application of the renewal of a licence to trade or of ongoing payment of business rates, business-related insurance premiums, employer National Insurance contributions or franchise payments to the parent company

- If the business is required to produce annual audited accounts, such accounts for the last full/last two full financial year(s)
- If the business is not required to produce annual audited accounts, unaudited accounts for the last full/last two full financial year(s) and an accountant's certificate of confirmation from an accountant who is a member of a UK Recognised Supervisory Body (as defined in the Companies Act 2006) or who is a member of the Institute of Financial Accountants, The Association of Authorised Public Accountants, The Chartered Institute of Public Finance and Accountancy, The Chartered Institute of Management Accountants, the Association of International Accountants or The Association of Accounting Technicians
- A certificate of VAT registration and the VAT return for the last full/last two full financial year(s) (copy or print-out), confirming the VAT registration number if turnover is in excess of £79,000 or was in excess of the threshold that applied during the last full financial year
- Evidence to show appropriate planning permission authority consent is held to operate or
- A franchise agreement signed by both parties (this is mandatory for franchise organisation)

Director or employee of a specified Limited Company in the UK

Company Tax Returns (CT600): Copies or printouts of the company tax returns for the last full financial year or the last two full financial years, along with evidence of filing with HMRC, such as electronic or written acknowledgment from HMRC

Registration Evidence: Proof of registration with the Registrar of Companies at Companies House

Annual Accounts: If the company is required to produce annual audited accounts, these must be provided for the last full financial year or the last two full financial years. If audited accounts are not required, unaudited accounts for the same period must be submitted, along with an accountant's certificate of confirmation from a qualified accountant who is a member of a UK Recognised Supervisory Body or other specified professional accounting bodies **Corporate/Business Bank Statements:** Statements covering the same 12-month or 24-month period as the company tax returns

VAT Registration and Returns: If the company's turnover exceeds £79,000 or the applicable threshold during the last full financial year, a certificate of VAT registration and the latest VAT return must be provided

PAYE and National Insurance Registration: Proof of registration with HMRC as an employer for PAYE and National Insurance purposes, including the PAYE reference number and Accounts Office reference number

Salary Evidence: If the director receives a salary, payslips and P60 (if issued) covering the same period as the company tax returns, along with personal bank statements showing the salary was paid into an account in the name of the director or jointly with their partner

Evidence of Ongoing Employment: Payslips and personal bank statements showing salary payments since the latest 12-month period covered by the company tax returns. Alternative evidence may include proof of ongoing payment of business rates, business-related insurance premiums, or employer National Insurance contributions

Dividend Evidence: If the director receives dividends, dividend vouchers for all declared dividends during or in respect of the period covered by the company tax returns, personal bank statements showing the dividends were paid into the director's account or a joint account with their partner, and evidence of ongoing receipt of dividends through dividend vouchers and bank statements

It is important to note that directors and employees of specified limited companies must rely on Category F or G to meet the financial requirements, as income from salary and dividends cannot be used under Categories A, B, or C. The relevant period for receipt of salary and dividends is the company's last one or two 12-month accounting periods, depending on whether Category F or G is relied upon Additionally, evidence of ongoing employment and/or self-employment at the time of application is required, as stipulated in Appendix FM-SE, paragraph 19(a).[33]

4. **Non-Salaried Employment (e.g., hourly paid)**

Non-salaried employment, as defined in Appendix FM-SE of the Immigration Rules, refers to employment where payment is made at an hourly or other rate, and the number or pattern of hours required to be worked may vary. It also includes employment where the amount paid

---

33 Minimum income threshold: Categories F and G—self-employment and directors and employees of specified limited companies - Minimum income threshold: Categories F and G—self-employment and directors and employees of specified limited companies > Specified evidence > Director or employee of a specified limited company in the UK

varies according to the work undertaken. This contrasts with salaried employment, which is typically paid at a fixed annual rate and is subject to a contractual minimum number of hours to be worked.

For non-salaried employment, Appendix FM-SE specifies that the gross annual salary at the date of application is calculated as the annual equivalent of either the gross income from non-salaried employment in the month prior to the application (if the employment has been held for no more than one month) or the average gross monthly income from non-salaried employment over a period exceeding one month prior to the application.

Paragraphs 18(d)–18(g) of Appendix FM SE introduce the concept of 'non-salaried' employment income, which is given as an acceptable alternative to 'salaried' employment, and provide how such income is to be calculated for the purposes of the Rules.

Calculation: Total gross earnings from the 12 months prior to the application are considered. This total must meet the required annual threshold.

To calculate the gross annual income from non-salaried employment as per Appendix FM-SE of the Immigration Rules, the method depends on the duration of the employment at the date of application.

If the person has been in non-salaried employment for more than one month at the date of application, the gross annual income is calculated as the annual equivalent of the person's average gross monthly income from non-salaried employment during the period prior to the date of application. For example, if the person earned £1,500, £1,600, £1,700, £1,800, £1,900, and £2,000 in the six months prior to the application, the average monthly income would be calculated as (£1,500 + £1,600 + £1,700 + £1,800 + £1,900 + £2,000) ÷ 6 = £1,750. The gross annual income would then be £1,750 × 12 = £21,000

If the person has been in non-salaried employment for one month or less at the date of application, the gross annual income is calculated as the annual equivalent of the person's gross income from non-salaried employment in the period immediately prior to the date of application. For instance, if the person earned £1,800 in the one month prior to the application, the gross annual income would be £1,800 × 12 = £21,600.

For weekly or daily payments, the calculation adjusts accordingly. For weekly payments, the gross annual income is calculated as the total gross income from non-salaried employment in the period prior to the date of application divided by the number of weeks and multiplied by 52. For daily payments, the gross annual income is calculated by dividing the total gross income by the number of days and multiplying by 365.

It is important to note that the calculated gross annual income can be combined with other permissible sources of income, such as non-employment income, pension income, or cash savings, to meet the minimum income threshold.

5. B. Non-Employment Income or **Cash Savings (Category D)**

For those not relying on earnings from work can rely on their cash savings as defined in Appendix FM.

Specifically, cash savings can be relied upon to meet the adequate maintenance test under Appendix FM, provided they meet certain evidential and procedural requirements.

To rely on cash savings, the applicant and/or their partner must have held the savings in their name or jointly for at least six months prior to the date of application. These savings can be transferred from investments, stocks, shares, bonds, trust funds, or proceeds from the sale of property within the six-month period before the application. However, the funds must be accessible immediately, even if there is a penalty for early withdrawal. The Immigration Rules specify that the savings must be held in a regulated financial institution and must be supported by personal bank statements and a declaration of the source of the savings.[34]

If the cash savings are derived from the sale of property, the property must have been owned by the applicant, their partner, or both jointly at the beginning of the six-month period and at the date of sale. Only the net proceeds of the sale, after deducting any mortgage, loan repayments, taxes, or professional fees, can be counted as cash savings. Additionally, the relevant period in which the funds must be held in cash can be reduced by the time elapsed between the start of the six-month period and the deposit of the sale proceeds into the account. The Immigration Rules also provide a formula for calculating how cash savings contribute to meeting the adequate maintenance test. The total qualifying cash savings are divided by the number of weeks of limited leave granted or by 52 weeks for applications for indefinite leave to remain. This weekly equivalent is then added to the weekly net income (before housing costs) to determine whether the financial requirement is met.[35] It is important to note that the evidential requirements for cash savings are stringent. Applicants must provide specified evidence, including bank statements, declarations of the source of savings, and documentation for liquidated investments or property sales. For example, if the savings are derived from the sale of property, evidence such as land registry documents, solicitor letters, or lender confirmations may be required.

Amount held as cash savings must be in an accessible account for a continuous 6-month period prior to the application date.

The amount needed is calculated using the formula: (£16,000) + (Required income shortfall x 2.5).

---

34 Appendix FM-SE Family Members – Specified Evidence, Cash Savings

35 https://www.gov.uk/government/publications/family-migration-adequate-maintenance-and-accommodation

Example (Partner visa at £29,000): If you have no income, you need: £16,000 + (£29,000 x 2.5) = £88,500 in savings.

Example (Topping up): If you earn £24,000 but need £29,000, your shortfall is £5,000. You need: £16,000 + (£5,000 x 2.5) = £28,500 in savings.

6. Pension Income

Pension income is categorised under Category E and can be used to meet the minimum income requirement of for entry clearance, leave to remain or settlement applications. Pension income can be State, occupational, or private that is in payment. In addition, War pensions, Armed forces compensation crime and Armed Forces Attributable Benefits Schema may also qualify provided that they are not excluded under Appendix FM-SE paragraph 21 (cc).

When calculating gross annual income from pensions, the pension must have been a source of income for at least 28 days before the date of application. However, exceptions apply if pension income is combined with self-employment income (Categories F and G) or salaried/non-salaried employment income under Category B. In such cases, the gross amount received from the pension in the relevant 12-month period is counted, rather than prospective entitlement. Furthermore, funds withdrawn from a pension fund or account within the last six months may be counted towards cash savings, provided specified evidence is submitted. The specified evidence required to demonstrate pension income includes official documentation confirming pension entitlement and the amount received, which may include documents from the Department of Work and Pensions, an overseas pension authority, or a pension company. Additionally, at least one personal bank statement from the 12-month period prior to the application date must show the payment of the pension into the applicant's account.[36]

Under Appendix FM-SE, paragraph 15(b)(iii), the gross amount received from a UK or foreign state pension or private pension by the applicant or their partner in the 12 months prior to the application date is considered part of the total income. However, pension income cannot be combined with specified savings to meet the minimum income threshold.

The Income Tax (Earnings and Pensions) Act 2003 provides further clarification on the nature of pension income and its taxation. Pension income includes pensions, annuities, and other types of income specified under various chapters of Part 9 of the Act.[37]

Errors in calculating pension income under Appendix FM can occur if the applicant fails to provide the specified evidence required under Appendix FM-SE. This includes official documentation confirming pension entitlement and the amount received, as well as at least one personal bank statement from the 12-month period prior to the application date showing payment of the pension into the applicant's account. Failure to provide these documents can result in the application being refused, even if the substantive financial requirements are met. Additionally, errors may arise if the pension income is incorrectly calculated using a financial year other than the tax year (6 April to 5 April), as clarified in the case of ***Hameed (Appendix FM – financial year).***

---

36 Minimum income threshold Category E-Pensions https://assets.publishing.service.gov.uk/media/691209e3e9348ac8fb54f4ba/Family+Migration+Appendix+FM+Section+and+Appendix+HM+Armed+Forces+Financial+Requirement.pdf

37 Income Tax(Earnings and Pensions Act 2003 (2003 C1) chapters 15A to 18 of part 9

Another potential error is combining pension income with other categories of income in a manner not permitted under the rules. For example, pension income cannot be combined with income from self-employment under Categories F and G, as the financial year for self-employment income is treated differently from the date of application for pension income. Similarly, pension income cannot be combined with specified savings to meet the financial requirements.[38]

7. Other Specified Non-Employment Income

This includes, but is not limited to:

- Rental income from property (minus mortgage/upkeep costs).
- Dividends or interest from investments, stocks, shares, or bonds.
- Maintenance payments from a former partner.
- Certain UK-based insurance or compensation payments.

C. Combined and Other Categories

8. Combining Different Income Sources (Category F & G)

You can combine multiple sources from the lists above to meet the total threshold, except you cannot combine cash savings with any other source unless it is salaried or non-salaried employment (Categories A & B only).

Common Combinations:

- Employment income + rental income.

---

38 Begum (employment income, Rule Article 8) {2021} UKUT 115 (IAC)

- Employment income + pension income.
- Self-employment income + non-employment income.

9. Benefits-Based Exemption (Category E)

If the sponsor receives certain specified UK disability-related or carer's benefits (e.g., Disability Living Allowance, Carer's Allowance, Personal Independence payment, attendance allowance, Care's Allowance or Armed Forces independence payment, they are exempt from the minimum income requirement. They must instead show they can provide "adequate maintenance" for the applicant and any dependants in the UK without recourse to public funds. Additionally, certain benefits, such as Personal Independence Payment, act as a "passport" to other benefits, including carer's allowance, disability premiums, and concessionary travel. These benefits also exempt households from the benefit cap, which limits the total amount of benefits a household can receive.[39]

Adequate Maintenance

A lower threshold where the sponsor must demonstrate they can support the applicant without recourse to public funds, based on current income after housing costs.

In accordance with the decision of the Asylum and Immigration Tribunal (as it then was) in *KA and Others (Adequacy of maintenance) Pakistan [2006] UKAIT 00065*[40]. "*The requirement of adequacy is objective. The*

---

[39] R (on the application of Ms C and another) v Secretary for Work and pensions (Zacchaeus 2000 Trust intervening)-[2015] ALL ER (D) 47 (Jun)- Judgement

[40] KA and Others (Adequacy of maintenance) Pakistan [2006] UKAIT 00065 (04 September 2006)

level of income and other benefits that would be available if the family were drawing income support remains the yardstick"

Paragraph 6[41] of the Immigration Rules sets out the definition of 'adequate' and 'adequately

"**Adequate**" and "**adequately**" in relation to a maintenance and accommodation requirement means that, after income tax, national insurance contributions and housing costs have been deducted, there must be available to the person or family the level of income or funds that would be available to them if the person or family was in receipt of income support."

The key requirement of the financial requirement is that the sponsor must maintain the partner with No recourse to public funds (NRFP).

Key Aspects of Paragraph 6 Public Funds[42]:

- **Definition:** Public funds comprise a precise list of welfare benefits and housing support, including Income-based Jobseeker's Allowance, Child Tax Credit, Council Tax Reduction, and Disability Living Allowance.

- **Excluded Support:** Certain, non-contributory, or emergency aid—such as NHS care, mandatory education, or some local authority emergency assistance—are generally not classed as public funds.

41 https://www.gov.uk/guidance/immigration-rules/immigration-rules-introduction

42 https://www.gov.uk/guidance/immigration-rules/immigration-rules-introduction#:~:text=%E2%80%9CPublic%20funds%E2%80%9D%20means%3A

- **NRPF Condition:** If a visa holds a "no recourse to public funds" condition, accessing these listed funds is a breach of immigration rules.

- **Devolved Benefits:** Paragraph 6 includes specific Scottish benefits like the Scottish Child Payment, Adult Disability Payment, and Child Disability Payment.

There is certain benefits that qualifies meeting the requirements of adequate maintenance and being exempt from earning of £29000 such as:-

Key Exemptions and Requirements:

- **Qualifying Benefits:** If the sponsor receives PIP, Disability Living Allowance (DLA), Carer's Allowance, Attendance Allowance, or Armed Forces Independence Payment (AFIP), they are exempt from the £29,000 threshold.

- **Test:** Instead of a set amount, the income must cover the household's expenses, including housing costs (rent/mortgage) and living expenses, effectively leaving them with an income at least equal to Income Support levels.

- **Exceptional Circumstances:** If the financial requirement is not met, the Home Office may grant a visa if a refusal would breach Article 8 (Right to family life) of the European Convention on Human Rights, such as causing "unjustifiably harsh consequences".

- **Documentation:** Evidence of the benefit award, bank statements for 6 months, and proof of housing costs (tenancy agreement/mortgage statement) must be submitted to prove adequate maintenance [43]

If the applicant's partner is in receipt of one of the above benefits or allowance on behalf of their child, the applicant will be able to qualify by meeting the financial requirement through adequate maintenance.

Calculating the minimum income

The Upper Tribunal in ***Ahmed*** formed a formula for calculating whether there will be adequate resources available at Paragraph 11:-

As adequacy of accommodation was out of the picture following the earlier decision, the present hearing was concerned solely with the maintenance requirement. Expressed mathematically, the formula to be fulfilled is

$A - B \geq C$[1]

where: A is the projected income what needs to be spent on accommodation and C the income support (or equivalent) figure (which we term in this decision "the benefit threshold")

Case Example Using £144.64 (Benefit Rate income support as of December 2025) Threshold

Scenario 1

Sarah makes an application for her husband to join her in the UK. She received a total weekly income of £310 after tax and national insurance been deducted her accommodation costs are £120 per week. The calculation is A £310 B Accommodation A-B +£190, C is income support level for a couple age 18 or over = £144.65 after deduction

43 https://www.gov.uk/uk-family-visa/proof-income-partner

Sarah's income exceeds the income support level therefore there will be adequate maintenance available.

Scenario 2: Higher Housing Costs

Sponsor receives PIP £172.75 a week, no other benefits and rent is £150 a week (no housing benefit) council tax is £30 a week his total income is £172.75.

Calculation

Needs £144.64 + £150 + £30 = £324.64 his net income is £172.75

Shortfall = £324.64 - £172.75 + £151.89 per week therefore fails to meet the adequate test.

Applicants must provide documentation as set out in Appendix FM-SE[44], clearly showing income, savings, or receipt of specified benefits.

Key Evidence Needed:

1. Benefit award letters showing all payments
2. Bank statements (6 months)
3. Rent agreement & payment proof
4. Council tax bill & payments
5. Utility bills (optional)
6. Savings statements (if applicable)

---

44 https://www.gov.uk/guidance/immigration-rules/immigration-rules-appendix-fm-se-family-members-specified-evidence

7. Proof of home ownership (if applicable)

Third Party Support

As outlined above the rules are drafted strictly in relation to meeting the financial requirements. Under the Appendix FM third party support is generally excluded (paragraph 1 (b) of Appendix FM-SE) however in certain circumstances third party support can be relied on. The rationale for excluding third-party support is that such promises are considered vulnerable to changes in the circumstances of the third party or the relationship between the applicant and the third party. However, following litigation, flexibility has been introduced under paragraph GEN.3.1 of Appendix FM to allow financial evidence from non-specified sources in cases where refusal would result in unjustifiably harsh consequences, potentially breaching Article 8 of the European Convention on Human Rights (ECHR). This provision is primarily aimed at the financial requirement rather than the adequate maintenance test, but it may be invoked in compelling cases.[45]

Under the exceptional circumstances provisions in GEN.3.1, third-party support can be considered if the applicant provides credible evidence of sustainable financial support from the third party. This evidence must demonstrate the genuineness, credibility, and reliability of the support, including its sustainability over the period of leave applied for. Factors such as the third party's financial situation, the nature and duration of their support, and the likelihood of changes in their circumstances or relationship with the applicant are assessed. The decision-maker has discretion in determining whether the evidence meets the required standards.[46]

---

45 Immigration rules Adequate maintenance –family members Guidance

46 Appendix FM exceptional circumstances cases under para GEN3, 149 Adequate maintenance and accommodation

In *MM (Lebanon) v SSHD*[47] the supreme court held the lawfulness of the rules regarding alternative sources of funding, including third party support but emphasised that the decision makers should not exclude reliable sources of earnings or finance altogether. The introduction of GEN.3.1 and para 21A of Appendix FM-SE has allowed for limited reliance on third-party support within Appendix FM itself, subject to strict evidential requirements.[48]

Documents Required to Prove Third-Party Support (In Exceptional Cases)

If you are relying on third-party support in an exceptional circumstance, you should include:

- A formal letter or statement from the third party confirming the support
- Proof of relationship to the sponsor or applicant
- Bank statements from the third-party showing ability to provide support
- A statutory declaration or affidavit
- Evidence of previous support (e.g., transfers, living arrangements)
- Evidence of income and expenses for the third party

47 https://www.supremecourt.uk/cases/uksc-2015-0011

48 *Mahad* (previously referred as AM) v Entry Clearance Office

If you are relying on third-party support in an exceptional circumstance, you should be aware that is discretionary and there are serious risks of refusal, such as:

- High risk of refusal unless exceptional circumstances are proven
- No guarantee that the Home Office will accept third-party support
- Potential delays or legal challenges
- May require an appeal or review

To succeed under GEN 3.1 is a "high threshold " ultimately it is for the applicant to prove that the refusal will breach article 8.

In the 2020 case of ***SD (British citizen children—entry clearance) Sri Lanka***, the Upper Tribunal found that the appellant, a Sri Lankan mother of two British children, did not meet the Immigration Rules despite providing evidence of an offer of employment in the UK on the grounds that she has 'not been able to show that there are exceptional circumstances, which could render refusal of entry clearance unjustifiably harsh' and that even if it were otherwise, the evidence fell short of what was necessary because, inter alia, the written offer of employment has not been witnessed or otherwise independently verified. As such, it was held that the refusal of her entry clearance application did not breach Article 8[49].

A factual example of third-party support in an Appendix FM application can be found in the case of ***SD (British citizen children – entry clearance) Sri Lanka – [2020] All ER (D) 127*** (the applicant, a Sri Lankan mother of two British children, provided evidence of an offer of employment in

---

49 https://www.gov.uk/guidance/immigration-rules/immigration-rules-appendix-fm-family-members

the UK as part of her application. However, the Upper Tribunal found that the written offer of employment was not witnessed or independently verified, and the evidence fell short of the required standard. Consequently, the refusal of her entry clearance application was upheld, as the applicant failed to demonstrate exceptional circumstances that could render the refusal unjustifiably harsh.[50]

It is important to note that the Home Office applies intense scrutiny to the evidence provided, focusing on the credibility, genuineness, reliability, and sustainability of the financial support. The applicant bears the burden of proving these factors to the decision-maker.

Risk Assessment

1. Initial Financial Questionnaire: Use a detailed form capturing all income sources, employment history, savings, and potential gifts.

2. For Category A/B clients, initiate evidence gathering 13 weeks before the planned application date. This identifies payslip gaps, bank statement issues, or employer non-compliance early.

3. The Source of Funds Narrative: For savings, draft a cover note pre-emptively explaining the origin, referencing the specific evidential documents (e.g., "The funds originated from the sale of a property in Mumbai, as evidenced by the completion statement dated 01/01/2023 and the subsequent bank transfer, shown on page 3 of the statements...").

4. Employer Liaison Template: Provide a draft letter for the employer, ensuring it contains every single piece of information mandated by the Rules.

---

50 https://tribunalsdecisions.service.gov.uk/utiac/2020-ukut-43

The rules are complex and evidence requirements are strict. Always refer to the official UK Government website Appendix FM 1.7: Financial Requirement guidance and the Immigration Rules for the definitive, up-to-date criteria before submitting an application.

Treat the financial requirement as a process to be engineered, not a hurdle to be jumped. Start early, document forensically, and think strategically about category selection. Your role is to translate the client's complex financial reality into the rigid, formulaic language of Appendix FM. The evidence must be so clear, so complete, and so logically presented that the caseworker's only possible administrative action is to tick the box marked "Met."

Red Flags

- Inconsistency: A 1p difference between the payslip net and the bank deposit.
- Unexplained Large Deposits in savings or personal accounts during the evidential period.
- Self-Employment with Historical Losses or income just below the tax threshold, suggesting non-viability.
- Cash Businesses with poor record-keeping.
- Using a Guarantor's Income. This is not permitted under the Rules.

Which financial requirement applies?

Type of application	Financial requirement

New application from 11 April 2024	£29,000
Renewal or extension from 11 April 2024 (including fiancés converting to partner)	£18,600 (plus applicant child increment*, capped at £29,000)
Pending application made before 11 April 2024	£18,600 (plus applicant child increment, no cap)
Sponsoring applicant in receipt of a specified benefit	Adequate maintenance based on current income support rates (see below)

*The child increment/s, where they apply are as follows: +1 child = +£3,800 for the first child and +£2,400 for each additional child, so eg +1 child = £22,400, +2 children = £24,800, +3 children = £27,200 and +4 children = £29,600 (unless capped at £29,000). British children and those with leave under Appendix EU are not counted for this calculation.

CHAPTER FOUR

ACCOMMODATION & ENGLISH LANGUAGE

Practitioners often treat accommodation and English language as "tick-box" items after the complexities of finance and relationship evidence. This is a critical error. These requirements, while conceptually simpler, are binary and absolute. Failure is not a matter of degree it is a flat refusal. This chapter provides the practitioner's framework for treating these areas with the same forensic rigor as the financial requirement, focusing on pre-empting caseworker doubt and navigating non-standard scenarios.

Under Appendix FM, an application for leave to remain as a partner is subject to the following requirement regarding accommodation.

> *E-LTRP.3.4. The applicant must provide evidence that there will be adequate accommodation, without recourse to public funds, for the family, including other family members who are not included in the application but who live in the same household, which the family own or occupy exclusively, unless paragraph EX.1. applies: accommodation will not be regarded as adequate if-*
>
> *(a) it is, or will be, overcrowded; or*
>
> *(b) it contravenes public health regulations*

Adequate Accommodation

The legal test as defined in the rules are more than just a roof. The Rules (Appendix FM, E-ECP.3.3.)[51] require that the applicant and sponsor will have "adequate accommodation" that is "owned or occupied exclusively by the family" without recourse to public funds, and that the accommodation will "not be overcrowded" under the Housing Act 1985.[52]

Adequate: means not statutorily overcrowded; in a reasonable state of repair; safe.

Exclusively Occupied: The couple must have the legal right to occupy it. Sharing with others is permitted if they have exclusive use of at least one room.

Overcrowding: A strict statutory calculation. The practitioner must perform this calculation.

The definition of overcrowding under the Housing Act 1985 is provided in section 324. A dwelling is considered overcrowded if the number of persons sleeping in the dwelling contravenes either the room standard specified in section 325 or the space standard specified in section 326. The room standard is breached if two persons of opposite sexes aged ten years or older (excluding partners) are required to sleep in the same room. The space standard is breached if the number of persons sleeping in the dwelling exceeds the permitted number, which is determined based on the number of rooms or the floor area of the rooms. Only rooms with a floor area larger than 50 square feet are considered, and kitchens,

---

51 https://www.gov.uk/guidance/immigration-rules/immigration-rules-appendix-fm-family-members

52 Housing Act 1985 (c68) Overcrowding

bathrooms, and toilets are excluded. Living rooms may be counted as bedrooms.

The Housing Act 1985 also provides a table in section 326(3)(b) that specifies the permitted number of persons for a given number of rooms or floor area. For example, one room allows two persons, two rooms allow three persons, three rooms allow five persons, four rooms allow seven and a half persons, and five rooms allow ten persons. For each additional room beyond five, two more persons are permitted. A child under the age of one does not count as a person for these purposes, and a child aged one to ten years counts as half a person.

Additionally, section 344 of the Housing Act 1985 includes an index of defined expressions for Part X, which references section 324 for the definition of overcrowding and section 326 for the permitted number of persons sleeping in a dwelling (see table below):-

Number of rooms available for sleeping	Number of persons permitted
1	2
2	3
3	5
4	7.5
5	10
an additional 2 persons for each room in excess of 5	

A child under the age of one does not count as a 'person' for these purposes and a child aged one to ten years will only count as half a person.

The Home Office Guidance Notes state:

> *"the accommodation can be shared with other members of the family provided that at least a part of the accommodation is for the exclusive use of the Sponsor and his dependents. The unit of the accommodation may be as small as a separate bedroom, but must be owned or legally occupied by the Sponsor and its occupation must not contravene Public Health Regulations and must not cause over-crowding as defined in the Housing Act 1985".*[53]

An illustrative case is *Rowe v Haringey London Borough Council,* where the Court of Appeal considered the application of sections 325 and 326 of the Housing Act 1985 in determining statutory overcrowding. The court clarified that overcrowding must be assessed based on the occupation of the dwelling as a whole. This case highlights the importance of landlords ensuring compliance with statutory provisions to avoid legal repercussions.[54]

Case law has clarified that statutory overcrowding under the Housing Act 1985 is relevant but not determinative in assessing the adequacy of accommodation for immigration purposes. In ***REHMAN v ENTRY CLEARANCE OFFICER, ISLAMABAD,***[55] the Tribunal emphasised that adequacy must be assessed based on the facts of each individual case, rather than solely relying on statutory overcrowding standards, the Tribunal noted that while statutory overcrowding provides guidance, the term "adequate accommodation" in the Immigration Rules is intended

---

53 https://assets.publishing.service.gov.uk/media/61b0a9c4d3bf7f05570653a8/Part_8_-_Family_members_Adequate_maintenance_and_accommodation.pdf

54 *Rowe v London Borough of Haringey* (2022) EWCA Civ 1370

55 https://tribunalsdecisions.service.gov.uk/utiac/2004-ukiat-6

to be assessed on a case-by-case basis by the entry clearance officer and appellate authorities.

Further, in ***Harouki v Kensington and Chelsea Royal London Borough Council,***[56] the court addressed the relationship between statutory overcrowding and the reasonableness of continued occupation under housing legislation. It concluded that overcrowding does not necessarily render accommodation unsuitable or unreasonable for continued occupation, even if it constitutes a criminal offence under the Housing Act 1985. This principle highlights the nuanced approach required in assessing accommodation adequacy in immigration cases, where statutory overcrowding may not automatically disqualify accommodation as adequate.

In summary, while statutory overcrowding standards under the Housing Act 1985 provide a framework for assessing overcrowding, the adequacy of accommodation in immigration cases is ultimately determined by the specific circumstances of each case, taking into account factors such as exclusivity of occupation, public health regulations, and the individual needs of the applicant and their family members.

Suggested evidence:-

- copy of the property deeds
- letter from the bank or building society as to the mortgage arrangements
- lease agreement and rent book—
- letter from the Local Authority or Housing Association

---

56 Harouki v Royal Borough of Kensington & Chelsea [2007] EWCA Civ 1000

- Letter from the family member or friend who is making the accommodation available to the applicant and their family unit.

- Utility Bills for the property including council tax bills showing the owner's name

- Proof of Homeowner's Identity: Passport copy

- Optional but Recommended: A short Property Inspection Report (can be done by the letting agent for a small fee) confirming the number of rooms, their sizes, and that the property is in a fit state.

Documentation is essential, regardless of any apparent financial capabilities of the sponsoring partner, to ensure the success of the visa application process.

For those who are sharing accommodation with other family members, the relevant Family migration caseworker guidance states that 'enquiries should be made about the number of rooms, the number of occupants and whether this is only intended to be a short-term arrangement'. The safest approach in all cases where the applicant is to live with the sponsoring partner in a shared family property is to include a letter from the head(s) of the household, evidence of their ownership of the property and confirmation of other occupants and the likely duration of the arrangement.

The Home Office caseworker guidance only explicitly recognises the possibility of 'prospective accommodation' in the case of persons applying for entry clearance as fiancé(e)s and proposed civil partners. However, even this apparent concession is narrowly drawn. In these cases, the 'decision maker must be satisfied that adequate permanent accommodation will be available after the marriage or the civil partnership has taken place and that adequate temporary accommodation will be available in the meantime, eg provided by family or friends.

Case Study: The Crowded House

Scenario: Sponsor lives with his parents and two siblings (aged 12 and 15) in a 3-bedroom house. Parents own the house.

Initial Assessment: High risk of refusal for potential overcrowding.

Practitioner's Action:

1. Measured Rooms: Bedroom 1 (master): 120 sq ft. Bedroom 2: 100 sq ft. Bedroom 3: 85 sq ft. Living room: 180 sq ft (not used for sleeping).

2. Calculated Capacity: Room 1 = 2 persons. Room 2 = 1.5 persons. Room 3 = 1 person. Total capacity = 4.5 persons.

3. Counted Household: Parents (2), Sibling 1 (1), Sibling 2 (1), Sponsor (1), Applicant (1) = 6 persons. Overcrowded by 1.5 persons.

4. Strategic Solution: The 15-year-old sibling was planning to move to university in 4 months, with evidence of an unconditional offer and student accommodation contract. The parents provided a letter confirming this planned departure.

5. Evidence Bundle: Homeowner letter, property inspection report, floor plan with sizes, overcrowding calculation showing current and post-departure occupancy (4.5 persons), sibling's university offer and accommodation contract. Cover letter explained the temporary nature of the current occupancy and the imminent change.

English Requirement under Appendix FM

The English language requirement under Appendix FM of the Immigration Rules applies to applicants seeking entry clearance or limited leave to remain as a partner.[57] This requirement is applicable to non-European spouses, civil partners, unmarried partners, fiancé(e)s, and proposed civil partners of British citizens or settled persons in the UK. The requirement also extends to spouses and partners of refugees and individuals granted humanitarian protection, as well as specified partners of members of the Armed Forces, in ***Bibi*** the Supreme court ruled that pre –entry English language requirement for foreign spouses is lawful and does not violate Article 8 ECHR, while the rule itself is justified the court expressed concern that the current guidance might breach human rights when compliance is practically impossible.[58]

To meet the English language requirement, applicants must provide specified evidence that they either meet or are exempt from the requirement. The ways to meet the requirement include: (a) being a national of a majority English-speaking country listed in paragraph GEN 1.6 of Appendix FM; (b) passing an English language test in speaking and listening at a minimum of level A1 or A2 (depending on the stage of the application) of the Common European Framework of Reference for Languages (CEFR) with an approved provider;[59] (c) holding an academic qualification recognised by Ecctis[60] (formerly UK NARIC) as equivalent to a UK bachelor's, master's, or PhD degree, taught or researched in English; or (d) qualifying for an exemption due to age (65 or over), physical or mental disability, or exceptional circumstances.

For initial applications, the minimum level of English required is A1 CEFR, which represents basic proficiency in speaking and listening. For extension applications submitted after 1 May 2017, applicants who have

---

57 https://www.gov.uk/uk-family-visa/knowledge-of-english

58 R (on the application of Bibi) (Appellant) v Secretary of State for the Home Department (Respondent) UKSC/2013/0270

59 https://www.gov.uk/guidance/prove-your-english-language-abilities-with-a-secure-english-language-test-selt

60 https://qls.ecctis.com/

already met the A1 requirement in a previous application must meet the higher A2 CEFR level unless exempt. Exemptions from the English language requirement are available for individuals who are aged 65 or over, have a physical or mental disability preventing them from meeting the requirement, or face exceptional circumstances.

For applicants who have previously met the English language requirement in a successful application, the Immigration Rules specify that they are not required to provide evidence again for subsequent applications for further limited leave to remain, provided the evidence submitted in the previous application still meets the current eligibility requirements [61]

Exemptions

Applicant's will be expected to meet the English language requirement if on the date of the application they meet one of the following criteria:

(a) They are aged 65 or over

Acceptable evidence of age includes a passport or travel document.

(b) They have a disability (physical or mental condition) which prevents the applicant from meeting the requirement

This exemption will only apply where the applicant has a physical or mental condition which prevents them from learning English or taking an approved English language test.

To qualify for this exemption, applicants must submit satisfactory medical evidence from a qualified medical practitioner which explains

---

https://assets.publishing.service.gov.uk/media/61b0aa758fa8f50380e90453/English_language_requirement_family_members.pdf the relevant physical or mental condition and why an exemption is justified.

(c) There are exceptional circumstances which prevent the applicant from being able to meet the requirement prior to entry to the UK

This exemption is only applicable where there are exceptional circumstances specifically relating to the applicant's ability to meet the English language requirement.

The applicant must demonstrate that, as a result of exceptional circumstances, they are unable to learn English before coming to the UK or it is not practicable or reasonable for them to travel to another country to take an approved English language test.

Examples of exceptional circumstances might include where the applicant:

- is a long-term resident of a country suffering armed conflict, or where there is or has been a humanitarian disaster for example in Afghanistan there are no test centres for female applicants

- has been hospitalised for several months immediately prior to the date of application

- is the full-time carer of a disabled child also applying to come to the UK

- is a long-term resident of a country with no approved A1 test provision and it is not practicable or reasonable for the applicant to travel to another country to take such a test

- is a long-term resident of a country in which the applicant faces very severe practical or logistical difficulties, which cannot reasonably be overcome, in accessing the learning resources required to acquire English language speaking and listening skills at CEFR level A1

Evidence of the nature and impact of the exceptional circumstances must be clearly provided, such as examples of previous efforts to access learning materials or to travel overseas to take an approved test and the obstacles to doing so. Lack of or limited literacy or education will not in itself be accepted as exceptional circumstances.

Test Format and Validity

Tests are designed to evaluate basic communication skills. The format typically involves:

- Short conversation with an examiner
- Describing familiar topics (family, work, daily life)
- Answering and asking questions

Each test certificate is valid for **two years.** If your application is submitted after the expiry date, you must retake the test — even if you previously passed it.

Common Refusals

One of basic refusal points very commonly is providing a certificate which isn't approved by the Home Office,

Examples:

- Taking a general IELTS test rather than **IELTS Life Skills A1** for Spouse Visa
- Booking a test at a centre not authorised for UK visa applications

- Using expired certificates
- Submitting a Degree without Ecctis verification report

Always make sure that you choose the centre from UKVI approved list. Check carefully the date on the certificates, apply to Ecctis early for a verification report. In case where you are requesting exemption please make sure you have made representations and provide medical report or disability exemption letter.

Eliminating All Doubt

The accommodation and English requirements are about certainty. Your evidence must eliminate any conceivable doubt in the caseworker's mind that the property is legally occupiable and not overcrowded, and that the language requirement is definitively met. By applying a rigorous, checklist-driven approach to these areas, the practitioner transforms them from potential minefields into straightforward components of a successful application.

CHAPTER FIVE

SUITABILITY REQUIREMENTS

For applicants and sponsors on the Partner route, the 2025 expansion of the suitability grounds represents a period of significantly heightened risk and scrutiny. Where refusal under these grounds was once primarily concerned with serious criminality or fraud, the changes introduced now cast a much wider net, directly impacting the assessment of "character and conduct" for both the applicant and, critically, the sponsor.

The core tension lies in balancing the right to family life (Article 8 ECHR) against the government's enhanced imperative to protect the public and the integrity of the immigration system. For couples, the actions of one partner can now more easily jeopardise the future of both.

From 11 November 2025, the suitability requirements for the Appendix FM partner route have been consolidated into the Immigration Rules[62], Part Suitability. This change was introduced through a Statement of Changes to the Immigration Rules. While the general suitability criteria under Part Suitability now apply to all family and private life routes, additional route-specific requirements remain in place for applicants under the Appendix FM partner route. These include restrictions for applicants with criminal convictions, involvement in sham marriages, use of false documents, unpaid debts to the NHS or Home Office, and breaches of immigration conditions during the qualifying period. Applicants who have entered the UK illegally must complete a ten-year qualifying period with permission under specified family/private life routes to be eligible for settlement.

62 https://www.gov.uk/guidance/immigration-rules

Key elements updated includes:-

- Criminal Convictions – Mandatory refusal for sentences of 12 months or more or discretionary refusal for lesser offences

- Immigration Breaches – Mandatory refusal re-entry bans for breaches such as illegal entry or overstaying

- Deception – use of false documents, misleading information or omission of relevant facts case result in refusal

- Non-conducive to public good – Presence in the UK is deemed undesirable based on character, conduct or association

The scope of the rules are established to apply in all cases except with some exception of Appendix EU, Asylum, appendix Settlement protection and Appendix Providers from Switzerland.

Under SUI 6.1, entry clearance under Appendix FM must be refused if the decision maker believes the applicant's parent or their partner pose risks to the child applicant. This is expected to be applied in cases involving children or dependent minors.[63] The long-standing 14 days grace period for late applications will continue under SUI 13.1, with allowances for good reasons beyond the applicant's control, as well as exceptions for those affected by Covid-19 pandemic and exceptional assurance.

The new suitability rules aim to ensure that only individuals of good character are eligible for settlement under the Appendix FM partner route. This includes stricter requirements compared to the previous

63 https://www.gov.uk/government/publications/suitability-false-representations-immigration-staff-guidance/part-suitability-deception-false-representations-false-documents-and-non-disclosure-of-relevant-facts-accessible

suitability criteria under Appendix FM, which were less restrictive in certain areas, such as immigration breaches and criminality thresholds. The suitability now applies to all Appendix FM applications and Human Rights based applications. In relation to partner's application the rules always contained flexibility where the applicants could proof exceptional circumstances such as breaches of article 8. However under the new rules these exceptions cannot override the certain part of suitability requirements if the applicants falls under any of these mandatory refusals such as where the applicant is subject to exclusion or deportation order. For example excluded under section 8B (4) of the *Immigration Act 1971*; excluded from the Refugee Convention, or convicted of a serious offence or persistent offending SUI 5.1. Although Appendix FM changes include transitional clauses for applications lodged before 11th November 2025, Part Suitability itself does not. This means even pre-11th November applications may still fall under the new regime if decided later.

When submitting an application under the partner route, you will usually in all circumstances include article 8 ECHR under old rules where submissions are made based on not meeting some of the requirements of the appendix FM such as English or financial requirements. The new rules have changes to these provisions so an application can only be granted on the basis of exceptional circumstances if the applicant doesn't fall foul of particular part of suitability provisions[64]:-

"*D-ECP.1.2A. Where paragraph GEN 3.2(3) applies but the applicant does not meet the suitability paragraphs SUI 2.1., SUI 2.3., SUI 4.1., SUI 5.1., in Part Suitability, the application on Appendix FM will be refused*"

An indefinite ban where there has been a custodial sentence of at least 12 months did not use to apply on this route. Under Appendix FM the absolute bar on settlement was set at four years, with 15 years needing to pass before a person with a 12-month+ sentence could settle. However,

64 https://freemovement.org.uk/new-suitability-rules-will-apply-to-appendix-fm-and-other-human-rights-applications/

this stricter requirement has been a policy change under the simplified routes.

Let's look at key changes with some examples below:-

a) The New "Prevention of Lawful Immigration"

This ground is particularly severe for partners who may have arrived in the UK via irregular means.

Scenario: If an applicant (or the sponsor) previously provided logistical or financial support to a family member or friend's irregular entry (e.g., a small boat crossing) before later applying for a partner visa, they could face mandatory refusal.

Impact: Even if the applicant is now applying perfectly lawfully from within the UK or overseas, their past "pre-existing conduct" in facilitating another's breach can lead to refusal. This applies even without a criminal conviction for smuggling.

b) Lower Criminality Thresholds – A Major Shift:

The most immediate practical change for many applicants.

New Threshold: The automatic refusal threshold for a custodial sentence is now lowered from 12 months to 6 months. A single sentence of 6+ months for either the applicant or the sponsoring partner now triggers mandatory refusal.

Example: An applicant with a historical 8-month sentence for a non-violent offence would now render their visa application ineligible for approval, whereas before it may have been considered under discretion.

Applicant and the Sponsor's Conduct: The rules explicitly require consideration of the sponsor and the Applicant's conduct and criminal record. A sponsor's conviction now directly threatens the application's success, not just the applicant's own history.

c) "Association" with Criminality – A Subjective Threat:

This broad new ground creates profound uncertainty for families.

How it Works: An application can be refused if the applicant or sponsor is "associated with" a person or group involved in crime, and this association is seen to "facilitate or lend support."

Partner Route Context: This could be invoked if a sponsor has close familial ties to individuals involved in organised crime, even if the sponsor themselves has no convictions. The Home Office could argue that family support (e.g., sharing a household) "lends support" to the criminal entity. This moves refusal grounds into the realm of perceived guilt by association.

d) Expanded "Non-Conducive" Grounds and Public Order:

The assessment of whether a person's presence is "not conducive to the public good" now explicitly includes:

Imposing a disproportionate burden on the NHS: A sponsor or applicant with a serious, long-term medical condition requiring very costly treatment could theoretically be assessed under this ground, though Article 8 claims would be strong.

Vexatious Litigation: If the applicant has a history of making multiple, manifestly unfounded immigration claims or appeals, this can now be cited as a specific reason for refusal under suitability.

e) Mandatory Refusal for Unpaid NHS Debt:

Previously a discretionary consideration, persistent, significant, or wilfully avoided NHS debt (e.g., from a previous visa period without immigration health surcharge coverage) is now a mandatory ground for refusal for a partner visa application.

The "Suitability" v "Eligibility" Trap

Applicants must understand this crucial distinction:

Eligibility: This is about meeting the positive requirements: relationship proof, financial requirement (£29,000 threshold from 11 April 2025), accommodation, and English language.

Suitability: This is the negative check. Even if every eligibility box is ticked perfectly, the application must be refused if the decision-maker is satisfied that one of the mandatory suitability grounds applies.

The 2025 changes have made this "suitability trap" both wider and deeper.

On 5th March 2026 the Home Office published a new statement of changes in immigration rules introducing a new suitability requirements and a new family life exceptional circumstances guidance[65]

Based on the Statement of Changes in Immigration Rules (HC 1691) published in March 2026, several new suitability requirements and tightened grounds for refusal for spouses and family members to take effect from **26 March 2026.**

Key changes include:

65 https://assets.publishing.service.gov.uk/media/69c279417e02b81c0d1c7746/Family_life_as_a_partner_or_parent_and_exceptional_circumstances.pdf

- **Suspended Sentences:** Mandatory refusal or cancellation of leave will apply to applicants who have received a suspended sentence of 12 months or more.

- **Expansion of Part Suitability:** The "Part Suitability" framework (previously introduced in Nov 2025) now fully applies to Appendix FM (family/spouse visas). This brings stricter, less discretionary scrutiny to applications regarding:

    - **Criminality:** Mandatory refusal for convictions resulting in imprisonment of 12+ months.

    - **Immigration Breaches:** Mandatory re-entry bans for previous breaches of immigration laws.

    - **Deception/Suitability:** Discretionary refusal for previous, less severe convictions, unpaid NHS debt, or fraudulent behavior.

Given the stricter scrutiny, preparation is more critical than ever:

· Disclose Everything: Declare all past criminal history (including spent convictions or cautions) and previous immigration breaches. Honesty is your best defense .

· Tie-Breaking on Article 8: If you have a criminal history, you must provide strong evidence of family life (e.g., British children, long residence) to argue that refusal would violate your Article 8 human rights.

These rules represent a shift toward more rigid enforcement.

Procedural Impact on Partner Applications

1. Enhanced Disclosure: The application forms now demand even more detailed historical information about associations, travel history, and past conduct from both parties.

2. Sponsor Scrutiny: The sponsor's CVRL (criminal record check) and full history are under a microscope. Any hint of "association" can trigger requests for extensive additional evidence.

3. Burden of Proof: While the standard of proof remains the "balance of probabilities," the types of evidence considered have broadened to include intelligence reports and open-source material (e.g., social media links to individuals of concern).

Legal Challenges and Article 8 on the Partner Route

The Partner route has the strongest statutory basis for an Article 8 ECHR 1950 claim discussed in more details in next chapter. Legal challenges will focus on:

Proportionality: Even if a mandatory suitability ground is met (e.g., a sponsor's 7-month old sentence), lawyers will argue that the devastating impact on family life outweighs the public interest in refusal, especially where children are involved.

Unjustifiably Harsh Consequences: Courts may be asked to intervene where the application of new grounds (like "association") leads to outcomes that sever family life for reasons perceived as tenuous or disproportionate.

Discrimination: There is a risk that assessments of "association" could disproportionately impact families from certain communities or regions.

Applications under the Appendix FM partner route can be refused or challenged on suitability grounds, which include issues such as previous immigration breaches, deception, or conduct deemed not conducive to the public good. For example, in the case of *R (on the application of Kucherov) v Secretary of State for the Home Department,*[66] the Court of

66 [2016] EWCA Civ 791, [2016] All ER (D) 36 (Aug)

Appeal upheld a mandatory refusal based on a re-entry ban due to a breach of visitor permission conditions by working in the UK. This case illustrates how breaches of immigration law, such as overstaying or using deception, can lead to mandatory bans and subsequent refusals under suitability grounds.

Another example is the case of *Iqbal (Para 322 Immigration Rules),*[67], which involved a refusal under paragraph 322 of the Immigration Rules due to the applicant's conduct. Although paragraph 322 does not apply to Appendix FM applications, similar suitability provisions exist under Appendix FM, such as S-LTR.1.6, which allows refusal if the applicant's presence in the UK is deemed not conducive to the public good due to their conduct, character, or associations *DK & RK (ETS: SSHD evidence; proof) India – [2022] All ER (D) 107 (Mar).*[68]

Additionally, in *R (on the application of Thebo) v Entry Clearance Officer Islamabad (Pakistan),*[69] the High Court considered a refusal of entry clearance under suitability grounds, highlighting the importance of addressing human rights considerations, particularly under Article 8 of the European Convention on Human Rights. This case demonstrates that even where suitability grounds for refusal are mandatory, applicants may challenge decisions on human rights grounds.

These cases underscore the broad scope of suitability requirements under Appendix FM, which can be difficult to challenge, particularly when mandatory refusal grounds apply. However, human rights considerations, such as the right to private and family life under Article

---

67 *Iqbal (Para 322 Immigration Rules)* [2015] UKUT 434 (IAC)

68 DK & RK (ETS: SSHD evidence; proof) India [2022] All ER (D) 107 (Mar)

69 R (on the application of Thebo) v Entry Clearance Officer Islamabad (Pakistan) [2013] EWHC 146 (Admin)

8 ECHR, may provide a basis for challenging such refusals – *DK & RK (ETS: SSHD evidence; proof) India – [2022] All ER (D) 107 (Mar).*

The Administrative Court in *R (on the application of Ngough) v Secretary of State for the Home Department* emphasised that a balancing exercise must be undertaken, weighing both positive and negative aspects of the applicant's character, conduct, and associations. For minor offences, greater justification is required to refuse an application under this ground, particularly if the offence is isolated. The reasoning behind the decision must be clear and focused, demonstrating a fair assessment of all relevant factors.[70]

Tips

1. Pre-Application Audit: Conduct a forensic "suitability audit" of both the applicant and sponsor's history: convictions, associations, financial dealings, and any potential involvement in immigration breaches (even tangential).

2. Proactive Mitigation: If a potential issue exists (e.g., a sponsor's old conviction), advice on preparing a detailed mitigation package upfront, including character references, evidence of rehabilitation, and a compelling Article 8 narrative including a detailed statement from both the applicant and the partner.

3. Full Candour: Never withhold information. Non-disclosure itself is a ground for refusal and will destroy credibility if a wider association is later discovered.

For the Partner route, the 2025 suitability grounds have fundamentally altered the landscape. The pathway to family reunion is no longer just about proving a genuine relationship and meeting a financial threshold.

---

70 *R (on the application of Ngough) v Secretary of State for the Home Department [2010] EWHC 2218 (Admin)*

It now requires navigating a minefield of broader conduct-based assessments that can render an otherwise perfect application doomed.

The system now explicitly communicates that the privilege of family life in the UK is contingent upon the perceived good character and lawful associations of both partners. Success depends on understanding these new hazards, keeping an eye on recent changes reported precedents and preparing applications with a level of thoroughness and caution that reflects this new, stricter era.

CHAPTER SIX

APPENDIX FM EX.1 AND ARTICLE 8 ECHR 1950

In this chapter we will explore a very specific area of UK immigration law. EX.1 and article 8 ECHR would typically cover the key "insurmountable obstacles" and "unjustifiably harsh test" for partners and connection with the right to private and family life.

Paragraph EX.1[71] has two sections one for partners and one for parents. In this chapter we will only explore on applications made by partners which is EX.1 (a) and EX.2 the test of insurmountable obstacles for partners which quotes "*The applicant's partner is in the UK and is a British Citizen… or present and settled in the UK and there are insurmountable obstacles to family life with that partner continuing outside the UK*".

EX.1. This paragraph applies if:

(a) (i) the applicant has a genuine and subsisting parental relationship with a child who-

- is under the age of 18 years, or was under the age of 18 years when the applicant was first granted leave on the basis that this paragraph applied;
- is in the UK;

71 https://www.gov.uk/guidance/immigration-rules/immigration-rules-appendix-fm-family-members

- is a British Citizen or has lived in the UK continuously for at least the 7 years immediately preceding the date of application; and

(ii) it would not be reasonable to expect the child to leave the UK; or

(b) the applicant has a genuine and subsisting relationship with a partner who is an eligible Sponsor, and there are insurmountable obstacles to family life with that partner continuing outside the UK.

EX.2. For the purposes of paragraph EX.1.

(b) "insurmountable obstacles" means the very significant difficulties which would be faced by the applicant or their partner in continuing their family life together outside the UK and which could not be overcome or would entail very serious hardship for the applicant or their partner.

Paragraph EX.1 under Appendix FM of the Immigration Rules provides an exception for certain applicants who are unable to meet specific requirements under the five-year route to settlement. It applies to partners or parents seeking leave to remain in the UK, but not to those applying for entry clearance. This exception is relevant in cases where the applicant cannot meet the financial, English language, or immigration status requirements of the five-year route, provided they meet all suitability and relationship requirements. However, applicants with valid leave as visitors or those with leave granted for six months or less. The test is not about choice, desire or difficult to leave. It sets a very high threshold, it is important to evaluate ties with UK vs ties to the country of return, health issues, presence of settled children in the UK, language/cultural barriers, safety and potentially the fate of settled partner/children in the UK. The threshold is deliberately set high in order to reflect the strong public interest in immigration controls. In effect as practitioner you must argue that the family life your client has established in the UK is not "portable" and cannot be exercised in country of origin. It is very important that at the outset you give your clients accurate legal advise as these cases are complex, fact sensitive where the quality of subjective and objective evidence is paramount. It is worth reading the Home Office guidance on exceptional circumstances which highlights key decision making process for applications made under EX.1.[72]

EX.1 leads to a 10 route to settlement, it is important to note that applicants relying on EX.1 must still meet the suitability and relationship requirements of the five-year route. The financial, English language, and immigration status requirements may be waived under EX.1, but the applicant must not have valid leave as a visitor or leave granted for six months or less, except in limited circumstances. Applicants on immigration bail or those who are overstayers may rely on EX.1, but this can have significant implications, including periods of overstaying, which may affect their application and future immigration status.

The case of *Sabir (Appendix FM EX.1 not free Standing)*[73] clarified that EX.1 is not a standalone provision but operates as an exception within other paragraphs of Appendix FM. This means that applicants must still satisfy other requirements of the relevant route under Appendix FM to benefit from EX.1.

Paragraph EX.1 under Appendix FM does not apply to entry clearance cases because it is specifically designed to operate as an exception within the framework of applications for leave to remain in the UK, rather than for entry clearance. The Immigration Rules explicitly state that EX.1 is not a standalone provision under which leave can be granted. Instead, it functions as an exception to certain eligibility requirements under the five-year partner or parent route for leave to remain, such as immigration status, financial, and English language requirements. However, it does

72 https://www.gov.uk/government/publications/family-life-as-a-partner-or-parent-private-life-and-exceptional-circumstance/family-life-as-a-partner-or-parent-and-exceptional-circumstances-accessible#Exceptional_circumstances

73 https://tribunalsdecisions.service.gov.uk/utiac/2014-ukut-63

not apply to entry clearance applications, as these are governed by different provisions within Appendix FM.

The rationale for this distinction lies in the structure and purpose of Appendix FM. EX.1 was introduced to address situations where removal of an applicant from the UK would breach the government's statutory duty under Section 55 of the Borders, Citizenship and Immigration Act 2009 to safeguard and promote the welfare of children, or Article 8 of the European Convention on Human Rights (ECHR). However, the Immigration Rules have been amended to include provisions for granting entry clearance outside the Rules in cases where exceptional circumstances or compassionate factors would make refusal a breach of Article 8. These provisions are found under paragraphs GEN.3.1–GEN.3.3 of Appendix FM, which explicitly address entry clearance cases and provide a framework for assessing Article 8 claims in such scenarios.

Arguments to support the application of EX.1 to entry clearance cases could focus on the overlap between EX.1 and the exceptional circumstances provisions under GEN.3.1–GEN.3.3. Both provisions aim to address situations where refusal would result in unjustifiably harsh consequences for the applicant, their partner, or a relevant child. Advocates could argue that the principles underpinning EX.1, such as the best interests of the child and the reasonableness of expecting a child to leave the UK, should also apply to entry clearance cases to ensure consistency in safeguarding family life and upholding Article 8 rights. Additionally, it could be contended that the exclusion of EX.1 from entry clearance cases creates an unnecessary barrier for applicants who face similar challenges to those applying for leave to remain, particularly where family life and the welfare of children are at stake.

In support of this argument, it is worth noting that the courts have recognised the importance of considering the proportionality of refusing entry clearance in light of Article 8. For example in cases of *R (on the application of Agyarko) (Appellant) v Secretary of State for the*

Home Department (Respondent)[74] *and in R (on the application of MM (Lebanon)) v Secretary of State* [75]

The Supreme Court emphasised the need for a complete framework to assess Article 8 claims within the Immigration Rules. This suggests that the principles underlying EX.1 could be extended to entry clearance cases to ensure a fair and consistent approach to family life assessments.[76]

The court in *R (on the application of Agyarko)* cited the leading decision of the European Court of Human Rights in *Jeunesse v Netherlands*[77] in which the Grand Chamber identified (at para 107) the following factors relevant when assessing the proportionality of the removal of a non-settled migrant from a contracting state where they have family members: (1) the extent to which family life would effectively be ruptured; (2) the extent of the ties in the contracting state; (3) whether there were 'insurmountable obstacles' in the way of the family living in the country of origin of the non-national concerned; and (4) whether there were factors of immigration control (for example a history of breaches of immigration law) or considerations of public order weighing in favour of exclusion. See also *Lal v Secretary of State for the Home Department [2019],*[78] *GM (Sri Lanka) v Secretary of State for the Home Department [2019] EWCA.*[79]

74 https://www.supremecourt.uk/cases/uksc-2015-0129

75 https://www.supremecourt.uk/cases/uksc-2015-0011

76 Halsbury's Laws if England (volume 57 (2023) paras 1-281 vol 57 paras 282-577

77 https://hudoc.echr.coe.int/eng#{%22itemid%22:[%22001-147117%22]

78 https://www.bailii.org/ew/cases/EWCA/Civ/2019/1925.html

79 https://www.bailii.org/ew/cases/EWCA/Civ/2019/1630.html

The five-stage test for Article 8 outside the Rules

The Explanatory Memorandum to HC 194 sets out the 'bold new approach' which the Home Secretary, Theresa May, hoped would constrain judges dealing with art 8 claims in immigration cases. It is worth quoting the passage at 7.2 in full:[80]

> "*The new Immigration Rules will reform the approach taken as a matter of public policy towards ECHR Article 8 – the right to respect for family and private life – in immigration cases. The Immigration Rules will fully reflect the factors which can weigh for or against an Article 8 claim. The rules will set proportionate requirements that reflect the Government's and Parliament's view of how individuals' Article 8 rights should be qualified in the public interest to safeguard the economic well-being of the UK by controlling immigration and to protect the public from foreign criminals. This will mean that failure to meet the requirements of the rules will normally mean failure to establish an Article 8 claim to enter or remain in the UK, and no grant of leave on that basis. Outside exceptional cases, it will be proportionate under Article 8 for an applicant who fails to meet the requirements of the rules to be removed from the UK.*"

In this way, the Government sought to cure the mismatch, observed by the House of Lords in *Huang*,[81] between the Immigration Rules and art 8, in that individual cases could well fail under the former but succeed under the latter. The further observation by Lord Bingham that migrants are not represented in Parliament, and that their interests have not been the subject of debate in Parliament, led the Government to have a debate on HC 194 in the House of Commons on 19 June 2012.

---

80 https://assets.publishing.service.gov.uk/media/5a7cb946e5274a2f304efb12/hc194.pdf

81 https://en.wikipedia.org/wiki/Huang_v_Home_Secretary

If an applicant cannot meet EX.1, they can still make a claim outside the Immigration Rules under Article 8. This is assessed using the famous *Razgar* and *R (Nagre)* case law, now formalised in the Rules at *Appendix FM, Section GEN.3.2,*[82] *(The "Five-Stage Test" from Razgar):*

1. Is there private/family life engaged? (Usually accepted if there's a genuine relationship).

2. Would the interference by the Secretary of State (refusal/removal) have consequences of such gravity as to engage Article 8? (Yes, if family life exists).

3. Is the interference in accordance with the law? (Yes, under the Immigration Acts).

4. Is the interference necessary in a democratic society for a legitimate aim? (Yes, for the economic well-being of the country & the prevention of disorder – immigration control).

5. Is the interference proportionate to the legitimate aim? This is the crucial question.

The decision-maker must balance the public interest in immigration control against the individual/family's circumstances.

The public interest is heavily weighted by statute (Section 117B of the Nationality, Immigration and Asylum Act 2002). It emphasises:

- The maintenance of effective immigration controls.

82 https://www.gov.uk/guidance/immigration-rules/immigration-rules-appendix-fm-family-members

- That little weight should be given to a private life/relationship formed when immigration status is precarious.

- That speaking English and financial independence are in the public interest.

In *Nagre*[83] the court held that if the applicant cannot meet EX.1, they are unlikely to succeed under Article 8 outside the Rules, unless there are compelling circumstances.

In MM the court emphasised that the "insurmountable obstacles" test is a high one, but it must be applied realistically and contextually, considering the reality of the couple's situation.

In *Agyarko* the Supreme Court clarified that "Insurmountable obstacles" is a stringent test.

For claims outside the Rules, the test is whether there are "compelling circumstances" sufficient to justify a grant. The "compelling circumstances" test is also a high threshold, not easily satisfied. It requires something over and above the standard reasons for refusal.

KO (Nigeria) the Supreme Court held that for parents, the "reasonableness" of expecting a child to leave is a self-contained question. It is not about the conduct or immigration history of the parent. The focus is squarely on the child.[84]

---

83 https://www.bailii.org/ew/cases/EWHC/Admin/2013/720.html

84 https://www.supremecourt.uk/cases/uksc-2016-0107

This approach aligns with the formulation in *Nagre*, which has been upheld in judicial scrutiny, such as in the case of *Haleemudeen SSHD v SS (Congo)*[85]

The Court in *SS (Congo)* also produces a list of considerations that may weigh against entry outside the rules:

> "*In deciding whether to grant LTE to a family member outside the United Kingdom, the state authorities may have regard to a range of factors, including the pressure which admission of an applicant may place upon public resources, the desirability of promoting social integration and harmony and so forth. Refusal of LTE in cases where these interests may be undermined may be fair and proportionate to the legitimate interests identified in Article 8(2) of "the economic well-being of the country" and "the protection of the rights and freedoms of others" (taxpayers and members of society generally). A court will be slow to find an implied positive obligation which would involve imposing on the state significant additional expenditure, which will necessarily involve a diversion of resources from other activities of the state in the public interest, a matter which usually calls for consideration under democratic procedures.*"[86]

Several key cases have addressed the application of Article 8 of the European Convention on Human Rights (ECHR) in the context of entry clearance spouse applications. These cases provide guidance on how the courts and decision-makers assess whether the refusal of entry clearance constitutes a disproportionate interference with the right to respect for private and family life.

---

85 https://www.supremecourt.uk/cases/uksc-2015-0168#case-summary

86 https://freemovement.org.uk/court-of-appeal-considers-proper-approach-to-family-cases-outside-the-immigration-rules/

The case of *Chikwamba*[87] is significant in the context of Article 8 of the European Convention on Human Rights (ECHR) in immigration law. It established that where the sole reason for refusing a human rights application is the requirement for the applicant to leave the UK to apply for entry clearance from abroad, the proportionality of such a requirement must be carefully assessed. The public interest in enforcing such a procedural requirement may be low, particularly if it would cause significant disruption or hardship, such as impacting the welfare of a child.

However, the relevance of *Chikwamba* v Secretary of State for the Home Department – [2008] UKHL 40 has been narrowed in subsequent case law and legislative developments. The Court of Appeal in *Alam v Secretary of State for the Home Department EWCA Civ 30* clarified that the decision in is only potentially applicable in cases where the refusal of leave to remain is based solely on the procedural requirement to leave the UK to apply for entry clearance. The court emphasised that the case law on Article 8 in immigration matters has evolved significantly since *Chikwamba*, particularly with the introduction of Part 5A of the Nationality, Immigration and Asylum Act 2002, which requires courts and tribunals to give "little weight" to relationships formed while the applicant was in the UK unlawfully.

In *Butt*,[88] the court reiterated the principle from *Chikwamba*, stating that it is only potentially relevant in cases where the refusal of leave to remain is based solely on the procedural requirement to leave the UK to apply for entry clearance. The court emphasised that the Immigration Rules carry significant weight in such cases, and the absence of insurmountable obstacles to family life continuing abroad is a strong factor against Article 8 claims. Furthermore, the court noted that relationships formed while the applicant was in the UK unlawfully are less likely to succeed under

---

87 Chikwamba v Secretary of State for the Home Department - [2008] UKHL 40

88 Butt v Secretary of State for the Home Department [EWCA Civ 189],

Article 8, as the public interest in maintaining immigration control often outweighs such claims.

Practical Tips

A strong EX.1/Article 8 case requires detailed, credible, and corroborated evidence:

For EX.1(a): Evidence of why relocation is impossible (e.g., medical reports, evidence of lack of family/ties in home country, country expert reports on danger, proof of complete societal alienation, strong evidence of social and economic ties, pregnancy)

For EX.1(b): Evidence of the child's life in the UK (school reports, NHS letters, evidence of friendships/extended family). An independent social worker report commenting on relocation and impact on the qualifying child.

For Article 8 outside the Rules: Evidence of "compelling circumstances" – e.g., very strong, long-established family life where a partner has a serious, degenerative illness making them entirely dependent; exceptional situations involving children with severe special needs where removal would be catastrophic, establish private ties evidence such as financial commitment i.e mortgage, well establish business.

The High Threshold

EX.1 is the primary route within the Rules for human rights claims in partner/spouse cases.

The thresholds of "insurmountable obstacles" and "unjustifiably harsh" are deliberately high to reflect the strong public interest in immigration control.

Success outside the Rules under Article 8 is exceptional and requires "compelling circumstances."

CHAPTER SEVEN

APPLICATION PROCESS AND MECHANISM

A flawlessly documented case can be refused due to errors in the digital application process. This chapter is the practitioner's technical manual for navigating the UKVI's online systems a landscape of rigid forms and unforgiving technical requirements. Mastery here is not about immigration law; it is about process engineering, digital hygiene, and risk mitigation in an adversarial interface.

Visa application forms

The prescribed forms are:

FLR(M)— for extension of limited leave to remain applications under Part 8 and under the five-year route to settlement in Appendix FM

FLR(FP)—for limited leave to remain applications under the ten-year route to settlement in Appendix FM

SET(M)—for settlement applications under the five-year route to settlement in Appendix FM and Settlement as a partner

The Foundation

For each application you must set up an online account using your firm's details to log in or your client's details. If using the applicant's email make sure that you advise the applicant to use a dedicated email. Create a new professional email address (e.g j.smith.application@gmail.com) solely for the visa process. This avoids key communication from UKVI being lost in a cluttered in box. Have the applicant share their login credentials for this email with the password so you can access it for them. You need to monitor for correspondence such is ECO emails, request for further information and decision letters. To create an account start at the Gov.UK website "apply to join family members in the UK" page. This will direct you to the UKVI Apply Service.[89] On this page you have many options, for example are you applying online from outside the UK, applying online inside the UK, or switching and extending. You must click on the right link. For partners abroad you must select the applicant's current country of residence. Also bear in mind to use a private browser window for each new application to avoid cookie or cache conflict. Before logging in, ensure you have a complete, organised PDF files of all the supporting documents for the applicant, structure your folder in your desktop in the following order:-

Applicant' s Name

1. Application forms

2. Checklist

3. Passports IDS

4. Financial Evidence

5. Relationship Evidence

6. Accommodation Evidence

7. Evidence of English

8. Evidence of TB if applicable

9. Correspondence

[89] https://www.gov.uk/uk-family-visa

10. Previous Refusal if application

The online form is an interrogation not a conversation, your answers must be precise, consistent and framed.

Section 1 of the form is applicant's details, name must be exactly as spelled in the passport inconsistency will lead to complications. For nationality check if the client has dual nationality use the one with clear travel history between the partners. It is very crucial to declare every previous UK visas. It is good practise to have a spreadsheet ready with previous visa types, application dates and reference numbers (GWF/UAN) if you fail to mention previous refusals this could lead to refusal on the basis of "false representation".

Section 2 of the form will require you to provide the details of sponsoring partner settled in the UK. The details again must be a precise match as mentioned in passport or travel document. Select the correct category i.e British citizen or settled person ILR. In addition to personal details you must provide details about the sponsor's employment and Finance including full address for place of work. If the sponsor is employed and as soon as you enter the salary the form will automatically generate further demand for corresponding evidence in slots later.

Section 3 will require you to provide evidence of relationship, How did you meet?" Be factual and concise. "Introduced by mutual friends at a social event in London, July 2022" or "Met via online dating application in March 2023."

"When did your relationship begin?" This is a legal, not emotional, question. For unmarried partners, it is the date relation established or cohabitation. For spouses, it is the date you entered a committed relationship leading to marriage. Be consistent with your relationship timeline narrative.

"Do you live together with your partner?" If the applicant is abroad, the answer is "No." The follow-up "Why not?" requires a clear, rights-based answer: "Because the applicant requires entry clearance to reside with me in the UK." If you have detailed statements from the applicant and the sponsor you can in some boxes say “please see attached statements”.

Section 4 the form will ask you which category of financial requirement the applicant is relying on. Make sure you select the correct category. For example if you select “category A” income from salaried employment the form will automatically in the slots ask to provide evidence of 6 months payslips, bank statements and letter from employer.

Section 5 the form asks questions about the accommodation, such as ownership and overcrowding, your answers must corroborated by evidence you upload. And finally before submitting the form do the final checks and print a PDF copy of form send it to the applicant to check as this is your record of what you are submitting because once the form is submitted and paid for you cannot change the answers, errors require cancelling the entire application, losing fees and starting all over again. Once you submit the form your next strategy is booking a biometric appointment for the applicant and uploading all the supporting documents. Practitioners must make sure that the biometric appointment centre is selected by the applicants as they will be well aware of geographical areas near to where they live.

Uploading – The system provides pre-named sections (e.g., "Proof of Identity," "Sponsor's Proof of Employment"). Use them. Uploading a bank statement in the "Additional Documents" section when there is a "Financial Evidence" and if you have statements from the applicant and sponsor upload them in relationship section. The golden rule is that all documents must be PDF, if more than 10MB compressed them to shrink the size. You can also combine the documents for example combine all 6 months’ payslips name it “sponsor’s pay slips”. In the additional document section, you can upload letter of legal representation. Link every document with correct file name, in the declaration section make sure that the declaration is signed and uploaded. It is also a good practise to upload a copy of the application form with checklist. Before uploading do a final check of your ZIP file and make sure you that:-

- All documents are readable (not corrupted, not upside-down).
- All pages are present (no missing bank statement pages).
- The chronological order of financial documents is correct.
- No personal, irrelevant documents are included (old payslips, unrelated bank accounts).

Immigration Health Surcharge (I H S)

Once the application is paid and submitting there is no point of return the system will automatically generate health surcharge,

The system will calculate this automatically based on the visa length (33 months for initial application). As of 6 February 2024, it is £1,035 per year. For 33 months: (£1,035 x 2.75) = £2,846.25.

The IHS Reference Number is generated upon payment. Record it immediately. You will need it for any enquiry. If the application is refused, the IHS is refunded automatically. The application fee is not. The application fees is paid in local currency if it is an entry clearance application and paid in British pounds for in country applications. It is good practice to advise the applicant to use the sponsor's credit card if possible as the credit care offer stronger section 75 consumer protection if there is a service failure.

After payment and uploads, the applicant is directed to book biometrics with a commercial partner (VFS Global or TLScontact overseas, in the UK).

VFS/TLS Portal: This is a separate system with its own login. You must create another account here.

Service Selection: Priority/Super Priority: Purchased here, not on the UKVI form. Availability is limited. Document Scanning Assistance: Usually unnecessary if you have uploaded correctly.

Keep My Passport: A valuable service allowing the applicant to retain their passport while the application processes.

Biometrics Confirmation: Once booked, the appointment confirmation is added to your document checklist. Upload it back into the UKVI portal.

Errors to Avoid

Form/Evidence Mismatch e.g., Form says Category B, evidence shows Category A. Refusal. Perform a pre-submission cross-check using the summary PDF.

Uploading Unreadable/Corrupt Files Caseworker cannot view evidence. Refusal. Perform the final ZIP download and audit.

Missing Mandatory Upload Slot e.g., Leaving the "Proof of Employment" slot empty. Refusal. The system may not prevent this. Use your declaration sheet as a final checklist.

Biometrics Booking Delay Application may be withdrawn if not booked within a set period Book the first available appointment immediately, even if a distant date. You can usually reschedule earlier slots later.

The evidential requirements for leave to remain applications by partners applying under Appendix FM and Part 8 can be complicated.

In *R (Bhudia) v Secretary of State for the Home Department* the Upper Tribunal (Immigration and Asylum Chamber) [90] held that the stipulation in the then hard copy application form FLR(M) that partner applicants should provide six items of correspondence of a certain type was unlawful (as being an inflexible requirement that should have been laid before Parliament in Immigration Rules).

The digital application is a test of procedural discipline. It removes discretion and exposes any weakness in preparation. By treating the portal as a precise, rule-bound system and applying a military level of checklist-driven process control, the practitioner ensures the strength of the case built is not undone by a technical oversight. The goal is a submission so clean that the caseworker's task is reduced to simple verification.

CHECKLIST OF DOCUMENTS AND INFORMATION

Applicant:

Sponsor:

Information needed:

1. Full name of applicant (and any previous names also known by)
2. Date of birth of the applicant
3. Current passport or other valid travel identity documents (applicant's current passport needs to have at least one blank page)
4. Copies of the photo page and any visa or entry stamps in their previous passports

90 https://tribunalsdecisions.service.gov.uk/utiac/2016-ukut-25

5. Biometric residence permit (if they have one) and E-visa

6. Details of any previous immigration applications the applicant has made

7. Copies of all previous immigration application refusals

8. Details of any criminal convictions

9. Applicant's parents' dates of birth and nationality

10. Applicant's national insurance number (if any)

11. A certified translation of any documents that are not in English

Proof of Finances:

Depending on how the sponsor meets the financial requirement:

If employed (salaried or non-salaried):

- 6 months' payslips
- 6 months' corresponding bank statements showing salary deposits
- Letter from employer confirming employment, salary, and duration of employment

If self-employed:

- Latest HMRC tax return (SA302) and tax year overview
- Audited accounts or accountant's letter
- Business bank statements for the last 12 months

- Company registration documents (if applicable)
- Invoices and evidence of ongoing business
- Bank statements for last financial year

If using savings:

- Bank statements showing savings held for at least 6 months
- Evidence of source of funds (e.g., sale of property, inheritance)

(Sponsor) (IF ON BENEFITS)

Minimum income requirement: £29,000 per year (unless exempt due to disability or carer's benefits).

1. Documents showing benefits received such as letters from DWP etc.
2. Council tax bill in sponsor's name
3. Proof of monies from a pension(s) (if applicable)
4. Non-work income (for example from property rentals or dividends) (if applicable)
5. 6 months Bank statements showing their income (from benefits)

Details and documents for sponsor:

1. Full name
2. Any previous names held

3. Dates the previous names were held
4. Reasons for the change
5. Date of birth
6. Nationality
7. Passport
8. Right to be in the United Kingdom (for example they are British)
9. Details of previous marriage if applicable
10. Evidence of marriages ending (for example a divorce certificate)
11. Evidence of financial support provided by the applicant to other family members such as children if applicable

Medical treatment (Sponsor):

Details of any past medical history in the U.K

Proof of relationship:

1. How the applicant met their partner
2. When the applicant met their partner (date)
3. When their relationship started (date)
4. How often they see each other
5. When did they last physically see each other in person (date)
6. When they got married (date)

7. Where they got married (location city/town/country)

8. How long they have lived together (if applicable)

   Documents:

   a. Chat logs from social media/texting

   b. Facebook print screens

   c. Email records

   d. Phone records relationship evidence

   e. Travel documents on visits to each other (such as flight tickets and bus tickets)

   f. Hotel booking and payment receipts from all holidays together

   g. Pictures throughout the relationship (description and date on the reverse) (all photos should be physical copies. The Home Office do not accept DVD, USBs etc).

   h. Marriage certificate

   i. Wedding photos (in colour)

   j. Divorce certificate (if applicable)

Children:

Applicant must provide information about all children (even if they're not applying):

1. Their name

2. Their nationality
3. Their date of birth
4. Their passport details
5. Who the child normally lives with
6. Any other people with parental responsibility the child
7. How the applicant is involved in their day-to-day life
8. The child's extended family
9. Any countries the child has visited or lived in
10. Birth certificate of children

Evidence of appropriate accommodation:

1. Evidence that there is enough space for them at the property they intend to live in the U.K
2. Tenancy agreement
3. A letter from the sponsor's council/housing association confirming they have no objection with the applicant residing at the property upon his arrival into the U.K

Supporting letters:

Supporting statements from the applicant and the sponsor. You can write about:

a. How the financial requirement is met

b. How the accommodation requirement is met

c. How the relationship requirement is met

d. The development of the applicant and the UK partner (sponsor) relation

e. That the sponsor promises to provide the applicant with both the finances and accommodation in order to satisfy the Immigration rules.

English language requirement:

English language test certificate (CEFR Level A1 from an approved SELT provider)

Note: Applicants may be exempt from the English language requirement if they are nationals of majority English-speaking countries, over the age of 65, or have a physical or mental condition preventing them from meeting the requirement.

TB test requirement if applicable:

TB test certificate

Immigration health surcharge (as of 30.07.2025):

1. This is a compulsory fee

2. This fee will be £2,587.50

3. This will cover the duration of the visa

Home Office fee (as of 30.07.2025):

1. £1846 compulsory fee

CHAPTER EIGHT

EXTENSIONS / SETTLEMENT

The partner/spouses are initially granted leave for 2.5 years (30 months), allowing them to live in the UK with their Settled/British partners. It is important that the foreign spouse/partner applies for extension of stay from within the UK prior to the expiry of their leave. The earliest that they can submit an application is 28 days before the expiry date of their current visa. It is crucial to diarise the expiry date of the current visa in order to avoid becoming overstayer, practitioners must not use the visa expiry date, calculate from the date the applicant entered the UK on a spouse visa, bear in mind applying too early can lead to refusal of application being classed as invalid. After completion of 5 years under this route the applicant becomes eligible for indefinite leave to remain (ILR). As discussed in our previous financial requirement chapter the income threshold increased to £29000 on 11 April 2024 however if an applicant was already on the five-year partner route or applied for a fiancé, fiancée or proposed civil partner before this change, they will still continue to be assessed the previous £18600 threshold.[91]

The eligibility requirements for extension since 2026 are covered within Appendix FM,[92] briefly that the couple are still in a genuine and committed relationship, they meet the financial and English requirements in addition they must proof that they have not breached

91 https://www.gov.uk/government/news/fact-sheet-on-net-migration-measures-further-detail

92 https://www.gov.uk/uk-family-visa/partner-spouse

any conditions of their leave during their stay in the UK and they are a person of good character.

Errors in your extension applications can be fatal, a refusal or invalid application can disrupt your lawful residence and reset your settlement clock which means that the applicant will not be able to apply for settlement until they have completed 10 years. Approval of initial entry clearance application does not guarantee an extension therefore practitioners must ensure to review the applicant's circumstances and allow time for evidence preparation and online submissions to manage the risk of a rushed application.

The English requirement increases from level of A1 to CEFR Level A2. There is a central new requirement which is evidence of cohabitation, the couple must prove lived together since the last grant of leave. If still at the same address, evidence is minimal if changed addresses evidence is required for each address lived in the last 2.5 years. The rules requires that the applicant and their partner have lived together "*in a relationship akin to marriage or civil partnership for last two years*". The evidence must be from at least three different official sources spread evenly over the 24 months preceding the application in both names of individually to the same address:-

- Joint tenancy agreements/mortgage statements
- Joint council tax bills
- Joint bank account statements showing active use for bills
- Joint utility bills (gas, electricity, water, broadband)

If individual evidence to the same address the following are considered as strong evidence

- Individual bank statements.

- Official HMRC/DVLA/DWP letters.
- NHS letters/GP registration confirmations.
- Payslips (showing home address).
- Electoral register entries.
- Insurance certificates (car, home, life).
- Telephone bills

If you were engaged with same applicant during initial entry clearance application, upon approval immediately brief the applicant on extension application, cohabitation requirements and instruct them systematically compile and collect one piece of evidence from at least three sources. Please note that a gap of 4–5 months in evidence for one source is acceptable if covered by other sources. Larger gaps require a credible explanation (e.g., one partner was hospitalised, with evidence) or if the spouse has worked away from home briefly.

In relation to financial requirements you can rely on income from the sponsor and the applicant, gross annual income must meet £29000 or £18600. As explained above this must be evidenced with payslips and employer letter. If the applicants have changed employment the practitioners should consider providing all payslips in the last 12 months and P60 for the last full tax year.

The application is submitted online using FLR (M) form.

The FLR(M) form is used by individuals seeking an extension of stay as the partner of a person who is present and settled in the UK or as the partner of a person with refugee leave or humanitarian protection. The analysis will address the legal standards, requirements, and procedures for such applications, including the duration of leave granted and the provisions for exceptional-circumstances.[93]

Under the FLR (M) application, leave to remain is typically granted for a period of 24 months under Part 8 or 60 months under Appendix FM, provided all requirements are satisfied.

Paragraph GEN.3 of Appendix FM provides for exceptional circumstances where the financial requirement cannot be met using specified sources. In such cases, the applicant may meet the minimum income threshold in whole or in part with non-specified sources.[94]

The test of "exceptional circumstances" is high one. It is not enough to demonstrate that one's circumstances are unusual or difficult, or that one *almost* meets the requirements of the rules. It is necessary to prove that the consequences of a refusal would be disproportionate and not justified by the public interest, such as that in maintaining effective immigration control.[95]

Once this form is submitted and fees paid, the applicant's status is protected under section 3C of the immigration act 1971 even if the biometric appointment is at a later date.[96]

---

93 https://www.gov.uk/government/publications/apply-to-extend-stay-in-the-uk-as-a-partner-or-dependent-child-form-flrm/apply-online-form-flr-m

94 https://www.gov.uk/government/publications/family-life-as-a-partner-or-parent-private-life-and-exceptional-circumstance/family-life-as-a-partner-or-parent-and-exceptional-circumstances-accessible

95 https://freemovement.org.uk/appendix-fm-exceptional-circumstances/

96 https://www.legislation.gov.uk/ukpga/1971/77/section/3C

Similar to initial entry clearance application a biometric appointment must be booked as a UKCAS service point and document uploaded beforehand in advance of the appointment using UKVCAS portal.

Application fee to renew a Spouse Visa UK is £1,048 for each person applying. Other costs include Health Surcharge: £1035 per person per year.

To renew a Spouse Visa takes up to 8 weeks to process. If you need a faster decision when extending a spouse visa, you may be able to pay an extra £800 to use the super-priority service for a decision by the end of the next working day or £500 to use the priority service for a decision within 5 working days.

Practitioner's FLR(M) Pre-Submission Checklist

- Cohabitation evidence compiled: 6 items from 3 sources over 24 months.
- Financial evidence gathered for Category B (current + last 12 months).
- A2 English language test passed and certificate valid.
- Application timing calculated (within 28 days of eligibility, before expiry).
- Any change of address evidenced.
- Previous application history and documents referenced.

Indefinite Leave to Remain

The final sprint point in a partner/spouse application is obtaining settlement under the 5-year route. Once 5 years are successfully completed under this route the applicant is eligible to apply for indefinite leave to remain in the UK. The application is done online using SET (M) form.[97]

The requirement for indefinite leave to remain as a partner are covered under section R-ILRP of immigration rules.[98] To make a valid SET(M) application, the applicant must be in the UK and meet the general threshold requirements, which include submitting a valid application in accordance with Part 1 of the Immigration Rules, meeting suitability criteria, and fulfilling the eligibility criteria unless an exception applies additionally, applicants must demonstrate sufficient knowledge of the English language and life in the UK. This includes passing the Life in the UK test and providing evidence of English speaking and listening ability at a minimum level of B1 CEFR, unless exempt due to age, mental or physical condition.

The English-language requirement for partners seeking ILR under Appendix FM or Part 8 is distinct from the requirements for entry clearance or limited leave to remain. Applicants who are under 18, over 65, or unable to meet the requirement due to a mental or physical condition are exempt from the English-language and Life in the UK test requirements.

The SET(M) application form is specifically designed for partners of British citizens or individuals settled in the UK. It is distinct from other settlement application forms, such as SET(O), which is used for other categories of settlement applications.

SET(M) is the culmination of the 5-year partner route. The stakes are highest here: a refusal can reset the clock. The requirements are a blend

---

97 https://visas-immigration.service.gov.uk/product/set-m

98 https://www.gov.uk/guidance/immigration-rules/immigration-rules-appendix-fm-family-members

of the familiar and new, with an emphasis on continuous residence, good character, and integration in the UK.

The core requirements are:-

- Continuous Residence: 60 months (5 years) in the UK as a partner, with no single absence exceeding 180 days in any 12-month period. More flexible than other routes, but patterns of prolonged absence can raise "intent to reside" questions.

- Still Meeting the Relationship Requirement: Ongoing cohabitation and a genuine relationship.

- Still Meeting the Financial Requirement: MIR (£29,000) must be met at the point of application (Category B typical).

- Life in the UK Test: Must be passed. A separate, mandatory knowledge test.

- English Language at B1 Level: Higher than A2.

- Good Character: No unspent criminal convictions, no immigration fraud

The life in the UK test is a multiple-choice test on British traditions, history, government and laws. It must be booked through the official government website. Practitioners must make sure applicants are familiar with study materials which are available online and a handbook exists for practice questions.[99] The past certificate does not expire and can be used later in a British nationality application. Practitioners must advise applicants to prepare and take the test way before they complete the 5 years requirement failing which means that they can only apply for

99 "life in the UK test 2024" Lawton and Ahmed

extension and will not be eligible for settlement. The requirement for English language jumps to B1, if the applicant has used a degree for previous applications the certificates are valid and no need to retest if exempt.

There is also a requirement for continuous residence. The applicants must not spent more than 180 days outside the UK in any rolling 12 months period during the 5 years. The form online asks for all travel dates, hence maintain a travel log sheet by scanning the passport entries. Absences of over 180 days in exceptional circumstances can be disregarded due to "serious or compelling circumstances" (e.g global pandemic, serious illness or work travels) strong supporting evidence must be provided. The SET (M) form is quite detailed. It asks for full 5-year employment, address and travel history. In addition to the document list provided above for FLR (M) application you must provide Life in the UK pass test notification, B1 English evidence, all passports covering the 5-year period and a good cover letter summarising facts, continuous residence and compliance.

The Good Character Requirements

In previous chapters we have touch base on suitability grounds which is relevant in each and every immigration application. In an application for indefinite leave to remain it is a key requirement. Any unspent convictions under the Rehabilitation of Offenders Act 1974 are likely to lead to refusal. You must declare all convictions, immigration offences and non-compliance with bail conditions. The practitioner's duty is to conduct a thorough review of the applicant's history. In the event of conviction consider applying for further leave to remain by delaying the settlement application.

For SET(M), the Super Priority Service (next-day decision) is often considered essential. The cost is high (£800-£1,000+) but provides certainty and allows immediate planning. Standard processing can take 6 months, during which the applicant cannot travel outside of the UK.

The Fiancé(e) Visa Path

We will briefly touch base on the Fiancé path as most of the requirements for entry clearance are the same as discussed in chapters above. the fiancé route is designed to enter the UK with a 6-month visa to marry / form a civil partnership. The applicants cannot work, access public funds and must switch to a spouse visa within the UK before the expiry of their visa. For initial application the applicants must proof that there is a genuine intent to marry, have a genuine relationship, and meet the financial/accommodation requirements. Please note No HIS is paid at this stage. Practitioners should advise the applicant to show venue booking, correspondence with the registrar, evidence of engagement such as purchase of rings, gifts etc. Once the applicant arrives in the UK they must give notice at a UK registry office to marry.(there is a 28-day wait, possible investigation for sham marriages). Upon registration of marriage a FLR (M) application should be pursued in country.

The practitioners should consider comparing costs and time to ILR (5.5 years) if applying under this route and paying twice for applications, marrying abroad and applying directly as a spouse is more cost/time effective. As a practitioner always recommend this route where marriage in the home country is legally impossible or unsafe.

CHAPTER NINE

REFUSALS / APPEALS

Refusals of leave to enter or remain on partner route will carry the right of appeal, being the refusal of a human rights claim.

Under Appendix FM of the Immigration Rules, partner route applications are considered 'implied' human rights claims. Consequently, applicants whose partner route applications are refused are eligible for a right of appeal under the Immigration Act 2014 appeals regime. This applies to all partner applications submitted under Appendix FM, regardless of whether the applicant had leave to enter or remain at the time of application. The sole ground for appeal is that the decision is unlawful under section 6 of the Human Rights Act 1998. It is important to note that refused applicants cannot apply for administrative review in these cases.

Section 82 of the Nationality, Immigration and Asylum Act 2002 (NIAA 2002)[100] provides a right of appeal in three circumstances:

- where the SSHD has decided to refuse a protection claim (section 82(1)(a), 2(a) & (b))
- where the SSHD has decided to refuse a human rights claim (section 82(1)(b)), or
- where the SSHD has decided to revoke a person's protection status (section 82(1)(c), 2(c)–(e))

[100] https://www.legislation.gov.uk/ukpga/2002/41/section/82

There is no definition of a human rights claim in NIAA 2002, s 82. Rather, 'human rights claim' is defined in NIAA 2002, s 113 to mean 'a claim made by a person to the Secretary of State at a place designated by the Secretary of State that to remove the person from or require him to leave the UK or refuse him entry into the UK would be unlawful under section 6 of the Human Rights Act 1998 (c 42) (public authority not to act contrary to Convention)'.

The key elements of an Article 8 ECHR human rights claim under section 113 were set out in the High Court decision *of R (Alighanbari) v SSHD,*[101] at para [70] and endorsed and updated in *MY (refusal of human rights claim)* Pakistan,[102] as follows:

- a claim not to be removed from or refused entry to the UK

- an assertion of facts that could constitute an existing or prospective private and/or family life, the interference with which Article 8 of the European Convention on Human Rights (ECHR) protects, and

- an assertion that removal or refusal of entry will interfere with that private and/or family life (ie that the, or a, basis upon which the claimant wishes to remain in the UK is the desire to maintain or build a private and/or family life)

In *MY (Pakistan) v SSHD* the Court of Appeal, upholding the Upper Tribunal, underscored that a human rights claim as defined by statute for someone in the UK refers to a claim that ECHR rights would be breached by removing the claimant from the UK, or requiring them to leave. In *R*

[101] https://www.bailii.org/ew/cases/EWHC/Admin/2013/1818.html

[102] https://www.bailii.org/uk/cases/UKUT/IAC/2020/89.html

(Mujahid) v First-tier Tribunal,[103] the Court of Appeal re-iterated the requirement in finding that no right of appeal lay in that case where the challenge was to the type of leave granted (in that case limited leave to remain rather than indefinite leave).

The Upper Tribunal has held that a Home Office interview, which took place in prison and in which the applicant provided answers demonstrating that she wanted to remain in the UK based on her private and family life, amounted to a human rights claim. The tribunal separately held that the applicant had been granted indefinite leave to remain in 1993 and the lack of evidence in the Home Office's files regarding this was more likely to be because of record keeping errors. It had been accepted by the Home Secretary that the applicant should have been granted indefinite leave. The case is *R (SG) v Secretary of State for the Home Department* JR-2025-LON-000242.[104]

The Home Office's caseworker guidance provides that applications made under certain enumerated provisions of the Immigration Rules are human rights applications and the starting point will be that there is a right of appeal against a refusal of such an application. The list includes most applications under Appendix FM and Appendix Private Life.[105] Until 30 September 2025, this list included long residence appeals, which are often a form of 'upgrade' appeal from limited leave to settlement. The caseworker guidance stated that there would not be a right of appeal where a person already held leave to remain on a human rights route, because they would not be expected to leave the UK at the end of their leave, but there would be a right of appeal if they held leave on another basis. From 30 September 2025, the caseworker guidance has been

103 https://www.39essex.com/our-thinking/news/upper-tribunal-clarifies-whether-right-appeal-ftt-arises-where-human-rights/

104 https://tribunalsdecisions.service.gov.uk/utiac/jr-2025-lon-000242

105 https://assets.publishing.service.gov.uk/media/68dd34c5dadf7616351e4cd6/Current+rights+of+appeal.pdf

amended to state that the Home Office will not notify people of a right of appeal if they hold any leave at all (except for 3C leave dependent on the application). This sudden change in position, removing a right of appeal for a route which has been in place for more than a decade, may be controversial and people may test the lawfulness of the Home Office's position through litigation. It is the First-tier Tribunal who is the final arbiter of its own jurisdiction.

In the event of a refusal, practitioners should consider the initial steps to challenge the decision, including submitting an appeal. It is important to prepare an immediate post refusal protocol to manage the client's expectation with no panic and take control, provide clear, written advise on options costs and probabilities, consider fresh application if the merits of succeeding the appeal is low. An appeal is brought to the First Tier tribunal through an online portal called HMCTS it has been in place since 22 June 2020 and was designed to improve the UK's court and tribunal services, First-tier Tribunal appeal procedure is governed by the Tribunal Procedure (First-tier Tribunal) (Immigration and Asylum Chamber) Rules 2014 (SI 2014/2604) and the practice directions of the Immigration and Asylum Chambers of the First-tier Tribunal and Upper Tribunal.[106]

For in country applications the deadline to appeal is 14 days and for applications outside of the UK a strict 28-day deadline.[107] It is crucial to lodge the appeal online to protect the client's position and then consider the challenges against caseworker errors in applying the rules, no evidence or omission on missing documents such as a sequence of 6 months bank

---

106 *SI 2014/2604 Tribunal Procedure (First-tier Tribunal) (Immigration and Asylum Chamber) Rules 2014 (SI 2014/2604)*

107 Based on the Immigration (Leave to Enter and Remain) Order 2000 (as amended), specifically Article 8ZB (often referenced in context with 8ZA regarding notice of decisions), rules regarding when decisions are "deemed to be received"

statements. The tribunal fees for lodging an appeal are £140 if requested to be heard orally and £80 for paper determinations.

The starting point will be understanding and highlighting the anatomy of a refusal letter, has immigration rules being considered, identify the core reasons and move to next steps.

In statutory appeals against refusals under Part 8, a distinction used to be drawn in s 85 of the Nationality, Immigration and Asylum Act 2002 between in-country and out-of-country appeals, regarding the evidence that could be considered. Post-decision evidence was allowed for the former, but for the latter only evidence relating to 'the circumstances appertaining at the time of the decision to refuse' was admissible. This distinction has been abolished by the Immigration Act 2014, drastically reforming the appeal structure of the 2002 Act. Now, in any appeal, the Tribunal 'may consider any matter which it thinks relevant to the substance of the decision, including a matter arising after the date of the decision', although if a 'new matter' is brought up the Tribunal needs the consent of the Secretary of State in order to consider it.

Common Grounds for Refusal

Financial – Recalculate, go through evidence again, provide missing documents;

Relationship – Strengthen by providing additional evidence of love and commitments between the couple include witnesses and further travel logs;

English /accommodation – If the level of English is not accepted take immediate action. Advise the applicant to retake another test. If there is an issue of overcrowding, immediately instruct an estate agent to prepare a housing report;

Additionally, applicants may need to provide evidence supporting their human rights claim, particularly if the refusal would result in a breach of

Article 8 of the European Convention on Human Rights, which protects the right to family life.

For applicants who have overstayed their leave, the Immigration Rules provide exceptions under Appendix FM, paragraph EX.1 or the exceptional circumstances provision in paragraph GEN.3.2. These provisions allow for the assessment of partner applications within the framework of Article 8 ECHR claims. If an in-country application is unlikely to succeed, applicants may consider leaving the UK and submitting a fresh application for entry clearance under Appendix FM. However, it is important to note that paragraph EX.1 does not apply to entry clearance applications, although entry clearance outside the Immigration Rules may still be requested.

Practical steps

- check the date of the refusal and diarise the deadline
- consider the reasons for refusal given, against the immigration rules, policy guidance, the copy of the application that was submitted and your client's instructions
- sit down with the applicant and take further instructions if the factual reasons in the refusals were not disclosed to you and you were not aware of it based on general grounds for refusal
- if newly instructed in the appeal take full instructions on the matter and its background
- explore alternative remedies and options apply
- if the applicant was interviewed as a part of the application process request the interview notes and submit a subject access request to the home office. In any case this request should be

made where there is a doubt about the applicant's immigration history

- if a decision is made to submit a fresh application the cover letter must address the previous refusal points by providing further evidence.

Excessive delay to decide an application with reasonable timeframe

There is an 'implicit obligation' on the Home Office to decide applications 'within a reasonable time' *(R (FH) v SSHD).* Arguments based on excessive delay or failure to decide an application within a reasonable time can be difficult to win, because they are closely linked with the allocation of government resources. What counts as a 'reasonable time' to wait for a decision is very subjective and will vary from case to case and between different kinds of applications. The reasonableness of delay will be case specific, for example a case where delay puts a child at risk may be contrary to the Home Office's child safeguarding duty under section 55 of the Borders Citizenship and Immigration Act 2009, which may inform the reasonableness threshold. The longer the delay the more scrutiny that the tribunal or court may apply, but as with other delay cases, it is usually very important to collect evidence to demonstrate the substantial prejudice that the delay is causing.

A delay that causes substantial prejudice can breach Article 8 of the European Convention on Human Rights *(Anufrijeva v Southwark).*[108] This can be a head of claim in its own right and can also be important as a basis for seeking damages for harm caused by unlawful delay. A good

108 Anufrijeva and another v Southwark London Borough Council; N v Secretary of State for the Home Department; M v Secretary of State for the Home Department [2003] EWCA Civ 1406

example of this is the case of *Husson v SSHD*[109] where the claimant was found to be entitled to damages for the two-year delay in issuing his Biometric Residence Permit. Another example is the case of *Said v SSHD*[110] where a family received damages for 'manifestly excessive' ten-year delay in granting their indefinite leave to remain applications.

Challenging refusal decisions outside of litigation

As with delay issues (above), it is possible to challenge problems with a decision outside of litigation. These approaches can rely on diplomacy and persistence rather than the firm time-line of litigation. These options may be particularly important if the issue is a repeating one, so re-applying is unlikely to help, there is no right of appeal and judicial review seems unpalatable.

Outside of litigation the main ways to challenge problems with a refusal decision are:

- •informal representations to the Home Office, if possible to the team responsible for making the decision
- •making a complaint to the Home Office
- •contacting a Member of Parliament
- •Pre-Action Protocol correspondence with the Home Office, ahead of issuing an application for judicial review

Where a decision is certified with no right of appeal, an application can be brought for judicial review against the certification. An application

109 Husson v Secretary of State for the Home Department [2020] EWCA Civ 329

110 *Secretary of State for the Home Department v Said [2018] EWCA Civ 627*

must be brought within 3 months of the date of the decision. It is important that practitioners familiarise themselves with the procedure rules. It is out of scope of this book to include the procedure.

In cases where judicial review is sought to challenge the certification, the applicant must first obtain permission to apply for judicial review. If permission is refused and the application is certified as totally without merit, the certification itself is not appealable. Instead, the applicant may seek permission to appeal against the refusal of permission for judicial review. If permission to appeal is granted, the substantive claim will be considered, and the certification will be treated as part of the procedural history rather than a separate issue.[111]

For refusals involving marriage certificates under the Marriage Act 1949, section 31(2)(a), the applicant may appeal to the Registrar General. The Registrar General can either confirm the refusal or direct that a certificate be issued.[112] If the refusal was based on frivolous representations, the person making such representations may be liable for costs and damages.[113]

---

111 *Wasif v Secretary of State for the Home Department; Hossain v Secretary of State for the Home Department* [2016] EWCA Civ 82

112 *Immigration and Asylum Act 1999 (1999 c 33) - 163 Refusal to issue certificate*

113 *Immigration and Asylum Act 1999 (1999 c 33) - 163 Refusal to issue certificate*

MORE BOOKS BY
LAW BRIEF PUBLISHING

A selection of our other titles available now:-

'A Practical Guide to Probation Breaches and Other Applications' by Mark Thomas
'A Practical Guide to Remarriage and Divorce' by Cordelia Williams & Claire Howard
'A Practical Guide to Privacy, Transparency, Reporting Restrictions and Closed Proceedings in the Court of Protection' by Laura Mannering
'Beaumont on Barristers – A Guide to Defending Disciplinary Proceedings (Second Edition)' by Marc Beaumont
'A Practical Guide to Payments for Environmental Services' by Ben Sharples
'A Practical Guide to the Law of Pregnancy and Maternity at Work' by Rebecca Thomas
'A Practical Guide to Redundancy – Second Edition' by Philip Hyland & Collette Moore
'A Practical Guide to International Issues for Scottish Family Lawyers' by Susie Mountain, Donna McKay, Ken MacDonald
'A Practical Guide to the Law on Deprivation of Liberty' by Ben Troke
'A Practical Guide to Rights over Airspace and Subsoil – Second Edition' by Daniel Gatty
'A Practical Guide to the Law in Relation to Inquests' by Ramya Nagesh
'A Practical Guide to the Construction and Rectification of Wills and Trust Instruments (Second Edition)' by Edward Hewitt
'A Practical Guide to Data Protection in Social Housing' by Clare Paterson
'A Practical Guide to Spousal Maintenance – Second Edition' by Liz Cowell
'A Practical Guide to International Parental Child Abduction Law (England and Wales)' by Dr Onyója Momoh
'A Practical Guide to Deprivation of British Citizenship' by Sean Ell
'A Practical Guide to Commercial Property Service Charges' by Rachel Garton
'A Practical Guide to Clinical Negligence – Third Edition' by Geoffrey Simpson-Scott (Geoff)
'A Practical Guide to the Rights of Grandparents in Children Proceedings – Second Edition' by Stuart Barlow

'The Electronic Communications Code: A Practical Guide – Second Edition' by Kerry Bretherton KC, James Castle, Mark Loveday
'A Practical Guide to the Independent School Standards – September 2023 Edition' by Sarah McKimm
'A Practical Guide to Estate Administration and Crypto Assets' by Richard Marshall
'A Practical Guide to Parental Alienation in Private and Public Law Children Cases' by Sam King QC & Frankie Shama
'Contested Heritage – Removing Art from Land and Historic Buildings' by Richard Harwood QC, Catherine Dobson, David Sawtell
'The Limits of Separate Legal Personality: When Those Running a Company Can Be Held Personally Liable for Losses Caused to Third Parties Outside of the Company' by Dr Mike Wilkinson
'A Practical Guide to Transgender Law' by Robin Moira White & Nicola Newbegin
'A Practical Guide to 'Stranded Spouses' in Family Law' by Mani Singh Basi
'A Practical Guide to Residential Freehold Conveyancing' by Lorraine Richardson
'A Practical Guide to Pensions on Divorce for Lawyers' by Bryan Scant
'A Practical Guide to Challenging Sham Marriage Allegations in Immigration Law' by Priya Solanki
'A Practical Guide to Digital Communications Evidence in Criminal Law' by Sam Willis
'A Practical Guide to Legal Rights in Scotland' by Sarah-Jane Macdonald
'A Practical Guide to New Build Conveyancing' by Paul Sams & Rebecca East
'A Practical Guide to Inherited Wealth on Divorce' by Hayley Trim
'A Practical Guide to Practice Direction 12J and Domestic Abuse in Private Law Children Proceedings' by Rebecca Cross & Malvika Jaganmohan
'A Practical Guide to Confiscation and Restraint' by Narita Bahra QC, John Carl Townsend, David Winch
'A Practical Guide to the Law of Forests in Scotland' by Philip Buchan
'A Practical Guide to Health and Medical Cases in Immigration Law' by Rebecca Chapman & Miranda Butler
'A Practical Guide to Bad Character Evidence for Criminal Practitioners by Aparna Rao
'A Practical Guide to Extradition Law post-Brexit' by Myles Grandison et al
'A Practical Guide to Hoarding and Mental Health for Housing Lawyers' by Rachel Coyle

'Stephens on Contractual Indemnities' by Richard Stephens
'A Practical Guide to the EU Succession Regulation' by Richard Frimston
'A Practical Guide to Solicitor and Client Costs – Second Edition' by Robin Dunne
'Constructive Dismissal – Practice Pointers and Principles' by Benjimin Burgher
'A Practical Guide to Religion and Belief Discrimination Claims in the Workplace' by Kashif Ali
'A Practical Guide to the Law of Medical Treatment Decisions' by Ben Troke
'Fundamental Dishonesty and QOCS in Personal Injury Proceedings: Law and Practice' by Jake Rowley
'A Practical Guide to the Law in Relation to School Exclusions' by Charlotte Hadfield & Alice de Coverley
'A Practical Guide to Divorce for the Silver Separators' by Karin Walker
'The Right to be Forgotten – The Law and Practical Issues' by Melissa Stock
'A Practical Guide to Planning Law and Rights of Way in National Parks, the Broads and AONBs' by James Maurici QC, James Neill et al
'A Practical Guide to Election Law' by Tom Tabori
'A Practical Guide to the Law in Relation to Surrogacy' by Andrew Powell
'A Practical Guide to Claims Arising from Fatal Accidents – Second Edition' by James Patience
'A Practical Guide to Asbestos Claims' by Jonathan Owen & Gareth McAloon
'A Practical Guide to Stamp Duty Land Tax in England and Northern Ireland' by Suzanne O'Hara
'A Practical Guide to the Law of Farming Partnerships' by Philip Whitcomb
'A Practical Guide to the Law of Unlawful Eviction and Harassment – Second Edition' by Stephanie Lovegrove
'A Practical Guide to Costs in Personal Injury Claims – Second Edition' by Matthew Hoe
'A Practical Guide to the General Data Protection Regulation (GDPR) – Second Edition' by Keith Markham
'A Practical Guide to Working with Litigants in Person and McKenzie Friends in Family Cases' by Stuart Barlow
'Protecting Unregistered Brands: A Practical Guide to the Law of Passing Off' by Lorna Brazell
'A Practical Guide to Secondary Liability and Joint Enterprise Post-Jogee' by Joanne Cecil & James Mehigan

'A Practical Guide to the Pre-Action RTA Claims Protocol for Personal Injury Lawyers' by Antonia Ford
'A Practical Guide to Neighbour Disputes and the Law' by Alexander Walsh
'A Practical Guide to Coercive Control for Legal Practitioners and Victims' by Rachel Horman
'A Practical Guide to the Law of Driverless Cars – Second Edition'
by Alex Glassbrook, Emma Northey & Scarlett Milligan
'A Practical Guide to TOLATA Claims' by Greg Williams
'A Practical Guide to Elderly Law – Second Edition' by Justin Patten
'A Practical Guide to Responding to Housing Disrepair and Unfitness Claims' by Iain Wightwick
'A Practical Guide to the Law of Bullying and Harassment in the Workplace' by Philip Hyland
'How to Be a Freelance Solicitor: A Practical Guide to the SRA-Regulated Freelance Solicitor Model' by Paul Bennett
'A Practical Guide to Prison Injury Claims' by Malcolm Johnson
'A Practical Guide to Advising Clients at the Police Station' by Colin Stephen McKeown-Beaumont
'A Practical Guide to Antisocial Behaviour Injunctions – Second Edition' by Iain Wightwick
'Practical Mediation: A Guide for Mediators, Advocates, Advisers, Lawyers, and Students in Civil, Commercial, Business, Property, Workplace, and Employment Cases' by Jonathan Dingle with John Sephton
'The Mini-Pupillage Workbook' by David Boyle
'A Practical Guide to Crofting Law' by Brian Inkster
'A Practical Guide to the Law of Domain Names and Cybersquatting' by Andrew Clemson
'A Practical Guide to the Law of Gender Pay Gap Reporting' by Harini Iyengar
'NHS Whistleblowing and the Law' by Joseph England
'Employment Law and the Gig Economy' by Nigel Mackay & Annie Powell
'A Practical Guide to Noise Induced Hearing Loss (NIHL) Claims' by Andrew Mckie, Ian Skeate, Gareth McAloon
'An Introduction to Beauty Negligence Claims – A Practical Guide for the Personal Injury Practitioner' by Greg Almond
'Intercompany Agreements for Transfer Pricing Compliance' by Paul Sutton
'Zen and the Art of Mediation' by Martin Plowman
'A Practical Guide to Adoption for Family Lawyers' by Graham Pegg

'A Practical Guide to Industrial Disease Claims' by Andrew Mckie & Ian Skeate
'A Practical Guide to Conducting a Sheriff Court Proof' by Andrew Stevenson
'A Practical Guide to Vicarious Liability' by Mariel Irvine
'A Practical Guide to Applications for Landlord's Consent and Variation of Leases' by Mark Shelton
'A Practical Guide to Relief from Sanctions Post-Mitchell and Denton' by Peter Causton
'A Practical Guide to Equity Release for Advisors' by Paul Sams
'A Practical Guide to Financial Services Claims' by Chris Hegarty
'A Practical Guide to Financial Ombudsman Service Claims' by Adam Temple & Robert Scrivenor
'A Practical Guide to Running Housing Disrepair and Cavity Wall Claims – Second Edition' by Andrew Mckie & Ian Skeate
'A Practical Guide to Holiday Sickness Claims – Second Edition' by Andrew Mckie & Ian Skeate
'Arguments and Tactics for Personal Injury and Clinical Negligence Claims' by Dorian Williams
'A Practical Guide to Drone Law' by Rufus Ballaster, Andrew Firman, Eleanor Clot
'On Experts: CPR35 for Lawyers and Experts' by David Boyle
'An Introduction to Personal Injury Law' by David Boyle

These books and more are available to order online direct from the publisher at www.lawbriefpublishing.com, where you can also read free sample chapters. For any queries, call us on 0844 587 2383 or email us at mail@lawbriefpublishing.com.

Our books are all generally in stock at www.amazon.co.uk with free next day delivery for Prime members, and at good legal bookshops such as Wildy & Sons.

We are regularly launching new books in our series of practical day-to-day practitioners' guides. Visit our website and join our free newsletter to be kept informed and to receive special offers, free chapters, etc.

You can also follow us on Twitter at www.twitter.com/lawbriefpub.

www.ingramcontent.com/pod-product-compliance
Lightning Source LLC
LaVergne TN
LVHW022057200926
848481LV00003B/961
* 9 7 8 1 9 1 8 2 4 1 3 0 3 *